"Camille has said she does not consider herself a chef, but she is my favorite chef in the world. I'm excited for the essence of La Buvette to be shared with the world!"

DANNY BOWIEN,
chef and co-founder of Mission Chinese Food

"What Camille is doing in Paris is amazing. Her book shows us that keeping it simple, trying new wines, and making food that's direct is all we need for a great experience. She is an inspiration."

ANDREW TARLOW,
owner of The Marlow Collective

"Being a restaurateur is not, as many think, a glamorous profession. In her book, Camille reminds us of why we do it. Because luck found us, and gave us something we adore to take over our lives. This book is for everyone who dreams about falling in love with daily life."

GILBERT PILGRAM,
executive chef-owner of Zuni Café

LA BUVETTE

TO VALENTIN

LA BUVETTE

RECIPES & WINE
NOTES FROM PARIS

CAMILLE FOURMONT
AND KATE LEAHY

PHOTOGRAPHS BY
MARCUS NILSSON

TEN SPEED PRESS
California | New York

CONTENTS

RECIPES

BUVETTE:
Dans certains établissements publics, certaines manifestations, petit local ou comptoir où l'on sert à boire.

A SPACE FOR LIVING

While the sound of scooters buzzing through Paris traffic echoes along narrow rue Saint-Maur, a small neon sign glows in a window lined with wine bottles. Inside, people pull up mismatched chairs around a few small tables while Camille Fourmont stands behind the bar, opening wine, slicing bread, and finishing plates of giant beans with olive oil and citrus zest. Some people stop by for a bottle to take home, some step in for a quick *apéro* before dinner, and others settle in for the night, drinking Camille's favorite cuvées and eating small bites of food until the shop closes.

This is La Buvette, Camille's *cave à manger*, a wine shop in which customers can stay and drink as long as they order something to eat. Most of the time, it's just Camille behind the counter, so she acts as a host, cook, bartender, confidant, dishwasher, and any other position that needs to be covered. Before opening, she walks around the corner to buy flowers or hops on her Vespa to pick up rice vinegar from Belleville. Once back, she ties back her long wavy hair and prepares the mise en place: pulling out cheeses from the refrigerator to bring to room temperature, placing a cutting board next to a stack of fresh bread, and lining up the ingredients for her simple menu. A wine delivery arrives, so she unloads boxes and restocks the walls with the kind of bottles you'd feel lucky to drink every day.

La Buvette is a shop built around wine, but it is also a space for Parisian living. People come to celebrate birthdays, or to get over a long day of work, or just because they need to take a moment for themselves. In this way, it's a public place that acts like an intimate one. Usually, the night starts out quietly, with a few couples sitting with glasses of something easy to drink before they leave for dinner, but it often becomes much more animated as the evening progresses. A group of Parisian friends has come into the shop for so many Wednesdays in a row that they earned a nickname the Wednesday Club. Nearly without fail, members of this unofficial club can get Camille laughing to the point of tears at their crazy adventures.

In Paris, as in all big cities, time is precious, but getting together for a glass of wine or a meal in an unpretentious style can happen without much planning. Serving food and wine thoughtfully and with care doesn't require a big kitchen (no one in Paris has one), or an impressive cellar, or even the most perfect-looking plates and glasses. Just be charming and gracious, Camille says, and the rest follows. In this book, she shares this casual Parisian style of eating and drinking with friends. Whether at La Buvette or cooking at home, she starts by looking for ingredients everywhere from the Chinese grocery stores of Belleville to the wholesale market of Rungis outside of town. Over the years, she has made friends with artisans and chefs who supply her with charcuterie, cheeses, and olive oil. Everything is presented in a relaxed style on plates and silverware found in flea markets around Paris and its suburbs.

In the traditional sense of the word, a *buvette* is not much more than a refreshment stand, a place to drink something to quench the thirst. Still, the idea behind a *cave à manger*, a wine shop for eating, isn't so different. A simple idea can go far in helping us come together and connect in a meaningful way. In sharing Camille's stories in this book of how she cooks, eats, drinks, and lives in Paris, we hope that it may inspire you to create memorable moments no matter where you live or how big or small the occasion.

—KATE LEAHY

INTRODUCTION

IT'S A MINUTE BEFORE five o'clock in the evening, and I'm rolling up the metal storefront gate that covers the front of La Buvette. It rumbles as it rises and is quite heavy—nothing like the soft curtains of a theater. But I always get this feeling in the minutes before unlocking the door that I'm a stage hand, setting up the mise-en-scène for the evening. Each night the story is always a little bit different, with new characters mixing with familiar faces.

La Buvette is just a tiny place on rue Saint-Maur, a street on the east side of Paris that goes on forever. The shop itself has no kitchen, yet there is something special about it. Mosaic-tiled floors, marble counters, and mirrored glass give it a sense of being part of a different era, a space that cannot be duplicated but is also not precious. Maybe it's because La Buvette is not so refined and perfect that people feel free to be themselves there, to laugh a little while sharing food and wine, to leave me postcards for my walls, to not take life so seriously. It's as if La Buvette has evolved into something bigger than what fits inside its walls.

I had been looking for a couple of years for the place that would become La Buvette, writing down precise ideas of the wines I wanted to pour and the food I wanted to serve in a *cave à manger* of my own. But every time I found a potential location, I had to change the original idea somewhat by extending it or squeezing it because the space was bigger, or smaller, or there was some reason that made me alter the essence of the project. During that time, I often passed a grocery near my flat in the 11*ème* (short for the 11th arrondissement—administrative district—though in French we abbreviate it and in English we just call it "the 11th"). The shop never seemed to be open—or sell much beyond a few sad-looking mandarins and some wilted heads of cabbage. Although I did not find the shop inviting, I admired the physical space of the building, with its worn surfaces and tiled floor that originated in the 1930s when it was a *crèmerie* (dairy shop).

One day in August 2012, while riding my bike back from the market, I saw a real estate sign in the window announcing 67 rue Saint-Maur was for rent. I hopped off my bike and called the number on the sign—and some-one actually answered! (This was unbelievable considering it was Sunday morning in France, and my expectations of a real estate guy answering a phone were not high). Before I knew it, the space I had been dreaming

about was mine. I didn't have much money, so I borrowed furniture from my parents, including a handsome wooden bar that my father had rescued from a neighbor's house right before they were going to cut it into firewood. My parents also gave me a couple of chairs they rescued from a favorite bistro in the Loire Valley that had since closed. Friends and family helped me prepare the shop, and by December, I opened officially, turning on the neon sign in the window that says *la buvette* in small, cursive letters.

In those days, the neighborhood didn't have nearly as many new restaurants and bistros as it does now, so my *"la buvette"* (a French term for "refreshment stand") was a curiosity. Of course, none of the neighbors missed the sad mandarins and limp cabbage from the previous shop, and before long, regular customers told their friends about the place, who told their friends. As more people discovered La Buvette through *bouche à oreille* ("mouth to ear"—a French expression that means word of mouth), the wooden bar my father had saved was lined with glasses and little plates of food as more people began to hang out with me and drink new styles of wine from around France and a bit beyond its borders.

"You only have the luck you deserve in life," my father says, and maybe he is right. While my road to La Buvette was not linear, I did get lucky along the way.

BEGINNINGS

I can see myself sitting at the long bar in the house where I grew up. The living room and kitchen were in the same open room, and the bar divided the two areas. Because my father is tall, the bar itself was higher than normal, and that's where I'd perch while doing homework. The back wall of the kitchen had a mirror, so even when my mum had her back to me, she could check on my progress without turning her head. When I was a little girl, I didn't know she used the mirror, so I thought she had a superpower that made it impossible for me to do sneaky things. But the mirror was also helpful for me. While I was too short to see what my mum was cooking when I stood beside her, I had an expansive view of the kitchen from my seat at the bar, and whatever I couldn't see directly was reflected in the mirror. "Are you making crêpes for dinner?" I would ask. "Are you making a cake? Can I help?" When I look back and think about this house, this is what I remember most.

Our family ate well, but my mum was not fancy about it; she had enough to think about while raising two children. Some meals were as simple as frozen fish sticks, a classic childhood kind of food. My mum also had a habit of saving recipes she found interesting from magazines, and some of those clippings I take inspiration from today. No matter what was on the table, however, we always sat down for dinner as a family to share a moment in our day. Being together was more important than what we ate, even though the food was good. As a kid, I was never allowed to say I didn't like to eat something, especially if I hadn't tasted it yet, and so I ate whatever was put in front of me. It's a rule that has served me well as a wine shop owner— ✓ ✓ taste everything before forming an opinion.

These memories were made in the Loire Valley countryside, about an hour's train ride away from Paris, but in a village small enough that my brother and I could walk to school. Yet while we lived in the countryside, my mum was totally and completely a *Parisienne*. Whenever we visited Paris, she would point out everything that excited her. "Look how great Paris is!" she'd say. "Look how beautiful it is! Look at all that's going on here!" She'd even take delight in entering a Métro station. "Can you smell that? God! This is *so* the smell of Paris!" On visits to the city, she would walk us through Le Palais-Royal, and my brother and I always ran around the Colonnes de Buren, an art installation of black-and-white columns, as if it were a playground. Even though I had a great childhood in the countryside, to my mind's eye as a kid, there was no better place to be in the world than Paris. Someday, I would live here.

When I was seventeen, I got my chance, moving to Paris to study Arabic. In one of the city's suburbs, I found a student flat near my classes. It was nothing more than a small room with a bed, a desk, and a kitchen the size of a closet—not the kind of place that would inspire one to think much about cooking. But because it was my first time living away from home, my mum gave me a notebook filled with her handwritten recipes as well as

LA BUVETTE

LA BUVETTE

recipes from other women who were important to me when I was growing up. Her idea was that I could write my own recipes into the book so that over time, I would have my own personal recipe collection. But to be frank, apart from developing a bit of an obsession with panna cotta (which happens to be the perfect thing to make in a tiny kitchen), I did not cook much while at university. Instead, I studied during the day, found a job working as an usher at a theater across the street in the evenings, and started exploring the city on days off.

Through my studies, I traveled to Damascus a couple of times, staying for a year on my second trip. It was the first time living far from home, and even though I wasn't focused on food in the same way as I am today, I still have crazy memories of Syrian spice markets where piles of za'atar, curry spice blends, and dried fruit were sold next to everything from paint pigments to artificially colored candies. There wasn't a culture of vegetable markets in the Syrian city, but every day a man pushed a trolley through the streets selling freshly shelled fava beans and carrots peeled and ready to cook. One of my favorite things to eat in Syria was a chicken kebab sandwich served with fresh cherries, a flavor combination that I am still dreaming about finding in Paris one day. In Damascus I learned new ways of looking at the world, and while I didn't know it at the time, this interlude away from France may have made me more open to taking an unexpected career path.

UN PAVÉ DANS LA MARE

After university, I found a charming apartment in the 20ème, an affordable district on the far east side of Paris surrounding the Père Lachaise Cemetery. Everything in my life was going well, except for one detail: I needed to earn a living, and it wouldn't be with an Arabic language degree. To train for a "real" career, I signed up for a course to become a bookseller and looked for work in the meantime.

While walking through my neighborhood, my boyfriend at the time pointed out a help-wanted sign in the window of a restaurant. "Me, a *waitress*?" I said, insulted. (To this day, I don't know why I had this reaction to waiting tables.) Despite my response, he pushed me through door, and before I knew it I was standing in front of Christophe Lebègue, the manager of Le Café Noir, asking for a job and stretching the truth about how much I knew about waiting tables (which was nothing). I got the job, but—as can be expected—my first day of work was a disaster. I assumed I would be asked to never return. Instead, Christophe surprised me. "If you can come back tomorrow and turn everything you did today upside-down, then this will work out," he said.

The next day I did exactly what he told me to do. I came back the day after and the day after that, each shift becoming easier as I learned how to take orders and deliver plates to tables. Before long, something unexpected started to happen: I began to look forward to work. Le Café Noir wasn't a famous place, just a respectable neighborhood restaurant. A collection of old coffee pots lined the walls, and the floor had the kind of tiles you see in bistros all over Paris. For lunch, we covered the tables with paper and switched to tablecloths for dinner. The menu changed every day, and while it was not exactly from the local market, it was always in tune with the seasons. Christophe noticed my enthusiasm and offered me a larger role in the restaurant, but I turned him down, believing that my "real" future still belonged in selling books—working at Le Café Noir was only something to help me earn a living until my real career could start.

One day Christophe sat me down again. "You want a real job," he said, acknowledging the bookselling course I had signed up to take. "But I feel like you have a talent for restaurants. Consider my offer to teach you how to be a manager."

In French, the saying *jeter un pavé dans la mare*—to throw a stone in a pond—implies a provocation, something that disrupts the calm. For me, the offer to work as a manager at Le Café Noir was a stone thrown into my life's plan. Restaurant work seemed to come naturally to me, and I began to realize that I loved my job. I took Christophe up on his offer and stayed for a couple of years at the restaurant.

A WINE AND FOOD EDUCATION

At this point in my life—my early twenties—I was learning about restaurants, but not about wine. I was actually a little shy about it, drinking a glass of Champagne only on my birthday. But I was at a time in my life when I was ready to learn something new, and had I become friends with a pastry chef or fallen in love with a bartender, I could have gone into baking or bartending. Instead, I met Danièle Gérault, a wine agent, and my life took another turn.

In 2008, the owners of Mama Shelter, a boutique hotel down the street, recruited me to join the opening team of a new restaurant. The hotel was unique for the 20éme, which doesn't see many tourists. Designed by Philippe Starck, the restaurant had a large bar, a lounge area, and a graffitied ceiling, and it was many times bigger and busier than Le Café Noir. Alain Senderens, the hotel's consulting chef, brought in Danièle to create the wine list and train us in serving wine.

With short-cropped gray hair and bright blue eyes framed by round glasses, Danièle soon became my mentor, not only training me in wine service but also taking me to tastings all over Paris. I was very intimidated at the beginning, especially when asked for my opinion, but Danièle told me to say whatever came to my mind. One wine reminded me of walking on the beach when the tide is out and the sand is covered by thousands of tiny shells. It tasted like a mix of sand and salt, something that a professional might just call "mineral." Instead I exclaimed, "Oh my God! It reminds me of being a kid, walking on a beach!" Did I sound ridiculous? "It's not so ridiculous," Danièle reassured. She told me to trust my judgment and pick my own words.

Danièle focused on the human side of winemaking, making the distinction between craft wines and wine made on an industrial scale. Most often these were made in a classic, conventional style (with commercial yeasts and modern winemaking methods in the cellar), but she also exposed me to my first wine made without commercial yeasts, filtration, or other manipulations—a style that is often called natural today. I was fortunate to have this education, especially now that in France many people feel they have to choose between drinking "classic" wine or "natural" wine before

they even know much about wine at all. But Danièle repeatedly told me that I have a nose and a mouth, and those are all the tools I need to decide if a wine is to my liking.

THE CENTER OF EVERYTHING

A couple of years later, I was offered an opportunity to manage a beautiful new brasserie, but my job crumbled after only a month. I was heartbroken. Until that point I had been lucky in my career, progressing with each new position, so I wasn't prepared for not even having a job. But I had heard about a restaurant on avenue Parmentier in the 11ème that was getting attention in the media. That's all I knew about Le Chateaubriand before I walked by with my résumé and saw the chef, Iñaki Aizpitarte, standing in front. Recognizing him from a photo, I introduced myself and asked if he was hiring.

"But you're a girl," he said. I couldn't read his face or tell whether he was serious, but he took my résumé, didn't look at it, and then offered me the chance to come in to work the next day. The following morning, I had a message on my voicemail from Iñaki: "Don't forget when you come this afternoon, the dress code is a white shirt and a three-day-old beard," he said. Was this a joke? What kind of place was this?

I soon learned that at Le Chateaubriand, everything was dictated by the cooks. There was no music in the dining room, so customers had to listen to whatever music the cooks wanted to listen to (at the highest level) in the kitchen. The food was even more singular. Because Iñaki was self-taught, he was free of many of the rules that more formally trained chefs become attached to. Flavors could be brutal, but they were also intuitive. One night we served an amuse-bouche of deep-fried, tiny gray shrimp dusted with tamarind powder, while another night we had an egg yolk cooked in simple syrup and brûléed like a meringue. Turmeric, fennel seeds, espelette pepper, and nori power became standard seasonings. Sometimes the flavors didn't work together, but more often they did, giving the restaurant a tense energy. We never knew exactly what was going to happen each night.

I worked at Le Chateaubriand for only a couple of months before I helped open Le Dauphin, Le Chateaubriand's wine bar next door. Designed by Rem Koolhaas, the space was stark and loud, framed by a marble bar in the center of the room where I bartended. Opening a new bar or restaurant is never easy, and this was no different. But while every night seemed to be a marathon of pouring wine and serving food, I was also aware that a line formed outside of Le Chateaubriand before dinner with people who had traveled from all over the world to eat there. Whoever didn't go to Le Chateaubriand would pack into Le Dauphin, which had also become a destination. It was not a cozy kind of place, but in the back of my head I knew how lucky I was to be there at that moment in time. I could have been running around some big brasserie delivering nondescript plates of food to bored customers, but instead I was in the center of the Paris dining world as it was going through a culinary transformation, opening up to new ideas from around the world.

Because of its reputation for food and natural wine, Le Dauphin helped me shape my opinions of the things I like to drink and eat. Some regulars would drink anything I suggested, trusting me to steer them in the right direction. By gaining the trust of people like Frédérick Grasser-Hermé, a food-world insider who has written dozens of cookbooks, I began to have the confidence to create a place of my own. I had my own opinions on wine and food and wanted a place to exercise them. Luckily, as I found out when I opened La Buvette, nothing was better than being my own boss.

A MAGIC PLACE

La Buvette started out being a place for the neighborhood, so I never expected people to come from all over the world, especially people who knew so much more about wine and food than me, from sommeliers in Paris, to chefs from London, New York, and San Francisco.

Some chefs would even ask to work with me behind the counter on special collaborations. I will never forget the time Julie Della Faille, who is now the chef of Le Verre Volé (see page 81), cooked lobsters at La Buvette. We boiled them in water from an electric kettle and then seared them in an industrial toaster (the kind you see at hotel breakfasts). It was a crazy thing to do, but it was also so memorable that I would do it all over again. And one warm May, my friend Daniel Baratier, the former chef and owner of Les Déserteurs (who has since founded L'Auberge Sur-les-Bois in Annecy), collaborated on an ice cream bar with me. I bought so many ice cream cones for the event that for a couple of weeks after, I ended up serving ice cream to neighborhood kids in the afternoon so the cones didn't go to waste. In this way, La Buvette has truly become a place for living, a place with a little magic that I can cultivate but not control.

Maybe, as my father suggests, I deserve the luck I found, but I was also helped along the way by family, friends, and mentors. This book is as much about them as it is about me. Most of all, it is about La Buvette, the world it inhabits on the east side of Paris, and the people who have come through those doors to share a moment with me.

For that, I am indeed lucky.

La seule arme que je tolère c'est le tire-bouchon
(The only weapon I tolerate is a corkscrew)

—JEAN CARMET

WINE

WHEN A NEW CUSTOMER walks into the shop asking for a wine list, I instead start with a conversation. What do you like to drink? Do you prefer red, white, or something in between? This chat does not take long, but it is important to me. The reason I created La Buvette is to connect with people, and nothing makes me happier than getting to know my customers and that they paid my shop a visit. It also helps me figure out what kinds of wines might make them happy.

Having a conversation before I pour a glass is also necessary because the wines I serve come from winemakers who are conscientious about how they treat the land and the grapes, never adding things that change the wine in an insincere way. Sometimes this means that a wine I sell might not taste anything like a "typical" wine from a region. It also may have changed in the bottle more than would be the case if I were dealing with a conventional product. Think of it like a visit to a cheese shop: the woman selling cheeses knows best how her cheeses are tasting that day, and if you ask for her advice, you will be pleasantly surprised. I know my wines well and I serve only what I like to drink; it is not any more complicated than that.

As I pour a glass, I may offer a short story about the winemaker who woke up one morning and decided to change his life and make this incredible wine, and my customer is going to think, "Wow—I like this wine, and now I know a little more about the human being who made it." This is more in line with how I like to drink wine: I don't spend as much time analyzing data on the perfect vintage or growing region—we want to drink good wine in simple ways. There are a lot of books about wine that are quite impressive, telling every detail of the terroir or grape or method of production. While this is not one of those books, the stories I share about the wines I love show my own informal wine education.

LA BUVETTE

TASTING WITH CONFIDENCE

I gained confidence in my ability to taste wine with the help of Danièle Gérault, whom I call my wine fairy godmother. Danièle began taking wine seriously in the early 1980s, when she worked in the movie industry. At long lunches with film crews, she started to notice that the most expensive bottles on the table weren't always the ones that tasted the best to her. To find out why this was so, she drove around the countryside in between movie projects, visiting winemakers so that she could learn how they made their wine. Even though not everyone took the time to talk to her, those who did deepened her passion in a profound way, inspiring her to change her career and become a wine agent. Today, it's rare to see Danièle without her Smart Car packed with bottles for her next tasting appointment.

From the beginning of her professional wine journey to today, she has always trusted in her ability to discern when something tasted good, a conviction she passed on to me. Even though she was the expert, she always let me make up my own mind about a wine, never putting her ideas into my head.

"Your story isn't the same story as mine," she once told me. "Some people love acidity, some people hate acidity. You can make your own opinion. You can be the punk. Trust yourself."

She also taught me to stay curious. Even today, she pushes herself to try different wines, closing her eyes when she picks a bottle from her cellar so she doesn't always reach for the same thing. "My life is not long enough to taste all that I want to taste," she says.

NATURAL WINE

It was with Danièle that I first tasted natural wine. She introduced me
to Domaine Gramenon and Domaine Léon Barral, two iconic biodynamic
producers, but rather than making a fuss about how they farmed their
land, she simply noted that they made wines with care. Then she let me
taste them and decide for myself if I liked them. In this way, she taught me
how to taste before making an assumption, so that I could have a broad
wine education.

I still believe today that the most important thing is not the church a wine
belongs to (whether it's natural or conventional) but whether the person
behind the bottle is working with faith in their convictions to make good
wine. Personally, I prefer natural wines, those bottles in which nothing has
been added and nothing taken away. Generally speaking, this means no
pesticides in the vineyard, no commercial yeasts, enzymes, or chemicals
in the cellar, no filtration before bottling, as well as many other details.
There is a high level of risk when making wine without the safeguards of
technology, but what is produced is much more alive. I serve natural wines
because I love how they taste, I respect the people who make them, and
I feel they are healthier for the environment and for the drinker.

Yet even though "natural" is the description that many people use to talk
about these wines, I prefer to think of them as craft wines made with
conviction, just as Danièle taught me. There are so many misconceptions
about natural wine, one of which is that the wine must be certified organic.
When it comes to how the grapes are grown, it is more important to ask
whether pesticides were used on the vines than if the grapes are certified
organic. Many of the winemakers I work with aren't certified, even though
they care for the land in ways that often go beyond what's required for
organic certification. Another way people try to define natural wine is to
focus on whether or not a winemaker added sulfur, which can prevent wine
from spoiling in the bottle. However, sulfur (or the lack of sulfur) alone does
not define a wine as natural, and some winemakers I support use a small
amount of sulfur. All wines contain sulfites at some level because they occur
naturally during the winemaking process, so even a wine made without
additions of sulfur will have a note on the bottle saying "contains sulfites."

No matter how the wine is made, it still needs to taste good. To me, natural wine does not imply "funky" or "weird," descriptions in English that do not translate in my brain to flavors. (To me, "funky" is a musical style.) Sometimes a natural wine is a little left of center compared with a wine made in a classic style, meaning that it may be a bit cloudy or fizzy or even a little oxidative. Yet it still needs to taste like wine. These wines are not "weird" or "funky" just for the sake of being different. I strongly believe that being enthusiastic about natural wine does not mean apologizing for faults. I also think it is okay not to love every bottle of natural wine you taste. By sampling different wines and remembering what you've tried, you can start recognizing the styles you like best.

Finally, while I favor natural wines, I feel as though it would be crazy to refuse a beautiful glass of something Danièle pours me because it doesn't fit with my idea of natural wine. No matter what you prefer to drink, it is better to stay open-minded and not *bouder son plaisir* (sulk your pleasure), meaning don't ruin your experience with fixed convictions just because a glass might not fit a rigid wine philosophy.

À BOIRE (TO DRINK)

In this book, I share stories of bottles that have played a role at La Buvette or have helped me in my wine education, either because they taught me something new or left a lasting impression. In many cases, I can remember exactly where I was the first time I drank them. As the natural wine revolution has spread across France and far beyond, Paris has become a central place for tasting them, especially in little shops that serve food, like La Buvette. The *cave à manger* tradition (see page 75) has made drinking wine in Paris more democratic and diverse.

Through the stories I share, I also address broader topics in natural wine today, such as orange wine (see page 168), forgotten French grapes (see page 124), and my love for cider (see page 139), among others. I also talk about the fleeting nature of great wine, of taking a moment to enjoy those special bottles that may never be replicated. Through these stories, it's as if we're standing at the bar at La Buvette, I'm pouring you a glass of something I love, and I'm telling you a story.

APÉRO   There is an official definition of *apéro* in the dictionary, but to me it is simply something to drink before eating. My earliest *apéro* memories come from when I was a kid and my grandfather would make a syrup out of the black currants he grew in his yard. It was a concentrated version of the crème you'd add to white wine to make kir, an old-fashioned *apéro*. The *crème* had a bit of alcohol, but as kids we were permitted to drink a drop of it diluted in a glass of water before we sat down for our Sunday meals together. Today, I feel that *apéro* can be a lot more fluid, meaning anything from the little glass of wine that I sip while cooking for friends to the cider I drink on a relaxing Sunday afternoon or the glass of something nice to drink while listening to jazz on a sunny summer evening at La Fontaine de Belleville when all the windows are open to the street. If I want to get together with a friend, I might just text, "Let's meet for *apéro*." We'll spend the first part of the evening with a little wine and then we'll either go our own ways or decide to prolong the evening and share dinner together.

Il vaut mieux l'avoir en photo qu'à table
(It's better to have his picture than to
have him around your table)

—FRENCH SAYING MEANING A FRIEND WHO LOVES FOOD
SO MUCH THAT HE EATS MORE THAN HIS SHARE

FOOD

MY WORKDAY AT LA BUVETTE begins by first tidying up the room, polishing and putting away glasses, giving the floor a mop, and cleaning the windows. On a mirrored wall panel, I write out the menu, which is nearly always a mix of my classic dishes—*gros haricots blancs et zeste de citron*, the "famous" giant beans with citrus zest that nearly everyone orders—as well as cheeses, charcuterie, and smoked tuna. The cheeses change all the time, but I always have something I love on hand, from a creamy triple-crème to something stronger and blue. Every week, I serve a terrine (page 107) with homemade pickles, and I also often have *saucisson sec*, a cured sausage that just needs to be sliced into coins when ordered.

La Buvette has never had a proper kitchen—just a refrigerator, a wooden cutting board, and a portable burner that I carry up from the basement when needed. But even though I have only a small counter behind the bar to slice bread and plate food, I can still compose plates that make people think, "Oh, I hadn't thought about that before." A lovely creamy cheese, such as Brillat-Savarin, is perfect alone. But sometimes I like to add a little something extra. Everyone knows the fresh Italian cheese Burrata, but coating Burrata with a dust made of mandarin peels turns the familiar into something memorable. Few things are better to serve without fuss than charcuterie, and while I always like to have good-quality *saucisson* on hand, I've also found that it's possible to make terrines and cured duck breast myself with a little planning.

CURIOUS ABOUT TASTING

In France, there is a countrywide government education program called *La Semaine du Goût*—Taste Week—that focuses on teaching kids to be more aware of the diversity of tastes and flavors in food. The program started in the late 1980s as a way to preserve a love for good-quality, well-made meals in the face of the expansion of convenience products and fast food. When we were kids, my brother and I loved it so much that we'd ask our mum to blindfold us so we could play La Semaine du Goût at home. She would offer us a taste of something, and we would have to dig into our flavor memories to figure out what it was. Sometimes a flavor was familiar but still out of reach, such as the time she gave me a taste of black olive, a flavor I knew by heart, but one that I couldn't figure out while blindfolded. Even though we played this game for fun, I believe that's when I started to pay attention to taste. Today, I still approach food and cooking with curiosity, wanting to discover new flavors.

Sometimes I buy an ingredient because I'm in a Japanese grocery store in the 2ème and see something that's new to me. What does black sesame seed powder taste like, and how can I use it? The only way to figure it out is to buy some to take home. Whenever I spend time walking around Belleville, a neighborhood filled with Chinese grocery stores, I buy a new vinegar or a few herbs and come home and experiment. This doesn't always work out to my advantage: one day on a trip to Japan, I tried to pickle very sour cucumbers and the result was absolutely inedible. Not all experiments end in success, but they still teach me something.

An expertly stocked spice shop can be another place to continue a taste education. I must have walked by Épices Roellinger, a spice shop founded by chef Olivier Roellinger in the 2ème, countless times. When I finally went in to have a look, I spent hours smelling an astounding variety of spices, discovering timut pepper, and learning about vanilla by smelling beans from all over the world in the shop's La Cave à Vanilles ("Vanilla Cellar"). By encountering new things, I started to combine different flavors in my head that I had never considered before. The same is true when I stop by one of the locations of Terroirs d'Avenir ("terroirs of the future"), a company that was one of the first to connect farmers with chefs in Paris.

The produce is always good quality, and I can find crazy different varieties of citrus in the winter and delicate berries in the summer. Being open to new flavors is how we teach ourselves to be better cooks.

Sometimes my inspiration comes less from new ingredients and more from the desire to recapture the taste of a favorite meal or dish at a Paris restaurant. At Le Bougainville, an old-school bistro not far from Épices Roellinger, I sampled a terrine of chicken livers speckled with pistachios and apricots, an idea I liked so much that it influenced the flavors of the terrine I now serve at La Buvette. I also love new-style bistros, like Le Cadoret in Belleville run by Léa Fleuriot, the chef, and her brother, Louis, who manages the front of the restaurant. After lunch one day, I had a chat with Léa about her crème caramel, which is perfectly silky and unfussy, and she kindly shared with me her recipe (page 186). Down the street from Le Cadoret is La Fontaine de Belleville, which stays true to an open-all-day Parisian bistro but with good coffee (it's owned by local coffee roasters Brûlerie de Belleville). I've done pop-up events in the space serving my Egg + Eggs (page 102), inspired by a classic bistro way of serving eggs. (But the simplest way to serve eggs in a bistro is to simply hard-boil them and let people can crack the shells directly on the bar.) In other words, not all taste experiments need to be revolutionary. Sometimes it's just about paying attention to notice when a certain version of a classic is really good.

SIMPLE COOKING

I mention tasting before cooking because I am an untrained cook. I use intuition to figure out how to make something, and I don't always succeed. What usually works out, however, are the flavors I compose in my head. After my first visit to Épices Roellinger, I infused olive oil with the vanilla I had bought, and I put it on goat cheese, topping the plate with crushed green peppercorns. After smelling the vanilla and green peppercorns in the shop, my brain connected with my tastebuds, giving me the intuition that these flavors would pair well together. Fortunately, people loved the goat cheese dish because I realized after three days of serving it I had forgotten to actually eat it myself.

All this is to say that even if cooking techniques are not something you feel confident in, you can get better by teaching yourself how to taste with an open mind. Paying attention to flavor allows me to know when something would benefit from a bit of flaky salt on top or a squeeze of citrus juice. It's also okay to ask questions, and I have learned a lot by asking chef friends why they do what they do. It was a revelation when a chef told me to make sure to bring meat to room temperature before cooking it; this way, the meat doesn't go into shock from the heat, and it cooks more evenly. Now, before I make pork rôti (roast) inspired by my visits to Belleville markets (see page 164), I always take the meat out of the refrigerator an hour or so before I begin to cook it. These little tips add up over time and help make me more confident in the kitchen.

& À MANGER (& TO EAT)

The chapters are organized around the food I serve at La Buvette, as well as the food I make at home for friends. Most of these recipes are appropriate to serve at any time, the kinds of things to eat when you're at home and hungry but curious to try something new. And because I love having a little treat in the afternoon and a sweet bite after a meal, I have dedicated a section to *le goûter*, the French version of afternoon tea, as well as to dessert. Before I cook, I always have a few basics on hand, such as pickles and other simple things that help me add flavor while cooking.

C'est dans les vieux pots qu'on fait les meilleures soupes
(It's in the old pots that we make the best soups)

—FRENCH SAYING

STYLE

I'VE ALWAYS BEEN DRAWN to objects that come with a story, which is one of the reasons that I fell in love with the old *crèmerie* that became my shop. From the beginning, I envisioned creating a place that shared not only what I like to drink and eat but also the vintage objects I've collected over the years. Today, the wall behind the bar is filled with little ceramics, coins, and illustrations given to me by friends or found at flea markets. I could happily spend all day arranging these various treasures in my shop. Even as a kid, I spent hours setting the table for fun, focusing on how the napkin should be laid next to the plate, how the silverware should be positioned, and turning the Duralex water glasses upside down to see the number on the bottom (kids in France like to say that the number on the glass reveals your age). Still, La Buvette is not a museum, but rather a place where you can eat with your hands, drink what you like, and relax for the evening. Sometimes customers tell me they feel as if they are in someone's home, and that's the kind of mood I want to cultivate.

Each night, I ensure that the mirrors are clean, the glasses are polished, and wine bottles are lined up straight before opening. On some days, I may go around the corner to pay a visit to Isabelle Charansol's shop, Variations Végétales, to buy fresh flowers to brighten up the shop. Just like when I was a kid, I am still a geek about the details, taking time to select knives and forks to use at the shop and to think about how the food I serve will look on various plates I've collected over the years.

At home, my kitchen also reflects my love for vintage. Under my kitchen window, I have an open shelf stacked with bowls and plates, making it easy to set the table with favorite tableware with very little planning. I take the time to choose a favorite plate or bowl or whatever will make my meal look a little nicer—even if I am by myself and no one would know if I were eating my meal out of a plastic storage container or take-out box. To me, how I enjoy my meal is directly impacted by how it looks before I start. For even a simple lunch, I set out a cloth napkin and pour water into a nice glass. When the food in front of you looks nice, I believe your brain starts telling you that it's going to taste good, too.

My love for seeking out secondhand goods started in childhood. From the time I was seven to when I was seventeen and about to move to Paris, my

44

family took part in our town's annual *brocante*, which is something similar to a yard sale in America. On the first Sunday of September, neighbors lined the alley behind the wall of our garden with tables filled with old belongings they wanted to sell. My father would wake my brother and me up early in the morning when it was still dark outside so we could save the spots next to our house for our family and friends. Once everyone set up their area, we spent the entire day together, sharing a huge picnic lunch, selling things we no longer needed, and looking for treasures from our friend's tables. My parents used the opportunity to empty their parents' attics, and my brother and I would pick out the clothes that no longer fit or the bikes and roller skates that we had grown out of and try to sell them ourselves. Although I looked forward to this day, I have to confess that I was not a good *brocanteur* (someone who sells secondhand goods): I usually spent more money than I made. (One year, I even bought my friend's Game Boy because my mum *always* refused to get one for me.) Even so, I credit this event for instilling in me a love of looking for treasures through discarded goods, thinking of new ways to use objects from the past.

VINTAGE SHOPPING IN PARIS

When I began to live on my own in Paris, treasure hunting for vintage goods became one of my favorite ways to spend a weekend. The best times of the year to go are in the spring and fall, when the weather is nice and informal sidewalk sales and flea markets pop up in neighborhoods all over Paris. Any kind of market can be an opportunity for treasure hunting, whether it's the small one next to the Marché d'Aligre or Les Puces de Saint-Ouen, the largest and most famous flea market in Paris. If I have time for it, I know that the farther outside of Paris I am willing to travel, the better the prices will be. Over the years, I've found that it's best to go in the morning when the *brocanteurs* have the best selection and the crowds are smaller. However, if I see something that I truly love, and it is too expensive, I will be patient, returning later in the day (or even weeks later) to see if the treasure is still there. Once I fell in love with a ceramic terrine mold shaped like a rabbit, but the price was a bit too precious for me to buy it at that moment. A month later, I visited the same market stall and saw that the woman still had the rabbit on display. I had a conversation with her and she gave me a better deal, knowing that I would willingly buy it that day if the price was just a bit lower.

I learned to navigate flea markets in an organic way, starting by going with my friend Alex. It was on one of those trips that I first encountered pieces from Verceram (see image opposite the table of contents), a ceramic company that had a factory right outside of Paris until it stopped producing in the 1970s. Rather than making practical items for the kitchen, Verceram specialized in art ceramics for middle-class French people who wanted to have a little bit of design in their homes, and I became a bit obsessed with it. Over the years, I've collected oversized bowls, light fixtures, and vases finished with the company's signature metallic glaze—the crazier the better. Anytime I visit a flea market, I always have my eye out for a new Verceram to add to my collection. But that is just my style, and it isn't for everyone. Part of the beauty of going to flea markets is finding something—antique linens, costume jewelry, plates, vintage buttons—that speaks to you loud enough that you want to collect it.

VIDE-GRENIERS ET MARCHÉS AUX PUCES (SIDEWALK SALES AND FLEA MARKETS)

There are many places to shop for vintage goods in Paris, but the ones I love the most are *vide-greniers* (sidewalk sales) and *marchés aux puces* (flea markets).

Vide-greniers (meaning "empty the attics") are sidewalk sales in which people sell old belongings to make room in their homes. The sales are run by neighborhood organizations that set the schedules and take care of the paperwork required to use the sidewalk. For the price of about twenty euros, you can rent two meters of sidewalk to "empty your attic" on the scheduled date. When I lived close to the restaurant Septime, I took part in a vide-grenier with friends. It was a memorable day for so many reasons, especially because it included a delicious tart from pastry chef Pierre Hermé (see page 145 for more of the story).

A *marché aux puces* is a flea market, which is different from a vide-grenier because the goods are sold by *brocanteurs*, professional resellers of used goods. A *brocante* can either mean a vintage market run by brocanteurs or the yard sales run by ordinary people, as it was in my town when I was a kid. Next to the Marché d'Aligre, the vintage market in which brocanteurs set up temporary booths and tables with treasures is often called a brocante, and it is a lot smaller than the famous Les Puces de Saint-Ouen.

A VISIT TO LES PUCES DE SAINT-OUEN

When Parisians say "Les Puces," it's possible that they are be talking about flea markets in Montreuil or Vanves. But often they're referring to the largest and most famous flea market of all, which is in Saint-Ouen, the neighborhood just north of the Périphérique (the highway that separates central Paris from the suburbs). Large enough to be its own city neighborhood, the flea market is divided into several smaller markets to make it easier to navigate. The stalls within the market are permanent, and some look like proper shops except most don't have a door. On my visits, I start at the triangle-shaped Marché Vernaison, which is one of the oldest markets within Les Puces, with charming alleys filled with everything from paper goods and light fixtures to tableware and various kinds of curios. (This is where I found my rabbit-shaped terrine mold.) Starting at the intersection of rue des Rosiers and avenue Michelet, Marché Vernaison is also one of the first markets you encounter when walking from the Porte de Clignancourt Métro stop.

For many years, Les Puces had the reputation of being full of nothing more than overpriced antiques, and younger generations didn't want to visit it, especially because the neighborhood around the Porte de Clignancourt Métro was a little rough. The people who sold the goods were generally older, and young people didn't want to get into the business. But today, there is more reason to make the journey from the center of Paris to Les Puces. Near one of the entrances to Marché Vernaison off of the avenue Michelet, Pauline Taboulet runs PittsBroc, her booth selling vintage jewelry and ceramics. Her selection caught my attention when I saw she also had a couple of Verceram pieces (she loves them, too), so we struck up a conversation about how she became a brocanteur.

"The past is very important to me," Pauline (pictured at right) said, explaining that she turned to selling vintage goods after working in a high-end fashion chain where she felt stuck selling expensive clothes that had no story attached to them. She grew up going to brocantes on weekends with her parents, who have always been collectors. When she was a little girl, she started collecting jewelry, a habit that eventually led to her current profession. Through word of mouth, she found a stall for rent in Marché Vernaison and she set up her shop. Every inch is filled with vintage mirrors, signs, or fashion items, mostly from the 1960s and 1970s. Stacks of purses next to figurines line the back wall, though her favorite section is a glass case displaying vintage designer costume jewelry. To me, brocanteurs like Pauline give new life to forgotten objects.

ON COLLECTING

Even though I am always looking for a new piece of Verceram to add to my collection, or maybe even another terrine shaped like an animal, I've found that when I set out looking for one specific thing, I never find it. The days when I have no expectations are when I find the most beautiful things, objects that meant something to someone once and can find meaning again. Perhaps this is one of the reasons that I love vintage shopping. Even when I don't find anything, I have immersed myself with the lives of others who came before me.

MISE EN PLACE

Here are the ingredients, kitchen tools, and basic recipes that make cooking easier and more flavorful. There are some ingredients I am particular about—salt, olive oil, and citrus fruit, for example—but I am not a princess. When cooking at home, I shop in a regular supermarket down the street from my apartment, where I often buy salted butter for bread or tinned anchovies and cream for a quick pasta for dinner.

INGREDIENTS

SALT

My favorite salt is Maldon sea salt, which I sprinkle on everything from Burrata to giant beans. It is perfectly flaky, dissolving on your tongue without tasting too salty and adding a little bit of crunch at the same time. (I am also a bit of a maniac about *when* I add Maldon salt, which is after the olive oil so the crystals don't dissolve before you can taste them.) When Maldon salt is a bit too pricy to use for everyday seasoning, I use fleur de sel, which in France is less expensive and doesn't dissolve quickly. For seasoning cooking water or other basic tasks, I use fine sea salt, such as La Baleine, but Diamond Crystal kosher salt or sel gris work just as well. For recipes in this book that call for "fine sea salt," La Baleine is a good choice. If you prefer to use kosher salt, the results will be slightly less salty.

BUTTER

My favorite type of butter comes with sea salt flakes already mixed into to it, which is something you can buy at an ordinary supermarket in Paris. In the United States, buy salted European-style butter, which has a higher butterfat percentage. I buy only salted butter, even for baking desserts. If you, like me, find that American butter is never salty enough, add a pinch or two of Maldon sea salt on top.

BREAD

At La Buvette, I buy large, golden-brown round loaves from Thierry Breton, the chef of La Pointe du Grouin, who also has a wholesale bakery. He leaves a big bag of bread in the back of the shop before I arrive, and I slice it to order. If I'm running low on bread during an evening, I pick up a few baguettes from the *boulangerie* down the street—I always ask for it *bien cuit*—"well cooked" and deeply golden. When buying bread, look for naturally leavened bread, such as levain or sourdough, with the darkest crust.

CITRUS

Citrus fruit, to me, is magical. The broad range of aromas from the peel alone is one of the reasons I always have different varieties of citrus at home and at the shop. Citrus peels hold the fruit's essential oils, so when you grate the peels or dehydrate them, they will transfer some of that aroma into food to which they are added. But every citrus is different. In Paris, the most amazing time for citrus is in the winter, when I can choose varieties from Corsica to Sicily. The mandarins I buy from Cédric Casanova (see Olive Oil, page 54) are so special that I scoop out the fruit to eat or to make juice, and I dry the peels to make dehydrated Mandarin Peel Dust (page 68). *Cedrat* (citron) is mostly skin and white, cottony pith; it has very little juice, but its rind smells floral and sweet, and I like to serve thin slices of *cedrat* with cured fish. Bergamot is another of my favorites for zesting, while pomelo has amazing pulp. No matter the citrus fruit you're using, if you are going to eat the peel (by grating it or drying it), buy organic citrus without a waxed rind to avoid eating pesticides.

NUTS

Hazelnuts from Italy's Piedmont region are my favorite nut to eat, and I keep a bag handy at home to use in everything from baking to topping pasta. Buying hazelnuts with the skin on is fine; peeling them off is too much trouble. I also love pistachios, sometimes using them as an alternative to hazelnuts (their green color looks charming when used on top of Goat Cheese, Black Garlic, and Cherries, page 98). Buy nuts in small quantities to ensure they stay fresh. If the nuts aren't toasted already, I just put them in a pan over medium heat and toast them for about 8 minutes (but I have to watch them to make sure they don't burn). Or I bake them at 300°F until aromatic, about 10 minutes.

OLIVE OIL

I discovered Cédric Casanova and his beautiful Belleville shop, La Tête dans les Olives ("the head in the olives") when I was bartending at Le Dauphin. A former tightrope walker, Cédric now focuses on importing olives, olive oils, and other Italian ingredients from Sicily, where he has family connections. Tasting olive oil at his shop is an incredible experience—some oils are powerful, others are discreet, and most are from single trees or farms. He names certain oils after the family who owns the orchard. When I opened La Buvette, Cédric started making an oil specifically for my shop from three old Biancolilla olive trees at the end of a field that had never been harvested for oil before. The following year the trees didn't produce enough olives, so he searched for other Biancolilla trees, and he has been making my olive oil ever since. The result is an oil that is not too strong or too discreet. I use it to coat Burrata, beans, and anything else at the shop that requires olive oil. At home, I use it to make a classic mustard vinaigrette for salad (page 115). For the recipes in this book, look for a well-balanced olive oil and skip the ones that are so grassy or peppery that they tickle the back of your throat.

PEPPERCORNS AND OTHER SPICES

Thanks to shops like Épices Roellinger, I am in love with peppercorns, especially timut peppercorns, which is actually not a true pepper. Timut has an amazing grapefruit aroma, and although it can be hard to find, it is worth seeking out at specialty spice shops. In its place, try Japanese sansho pepper, which has a similar citrus aroma as well. I also buy good-quality black peppercorns that I grind when I need them. And if you prefer food a little spicier, keep a small jar of red espelette pepper handy (though I confess that I am allergic to chiles). For any other spice I might use, I buy them in small quantities and store them in sealed containers so they keep their freshness.

DRIED HERBS AND DRIED FLOWERS

It is easy to dry your own herbs and leaves, from sage, oregano, and thyme sprigs to fig, nettle, and verbena leaves; hang a fresh bundle in the kitchen until the leaves are dry enough that they crumble when crushed with your fingers; this takes anywhere from 5 days to a little more than 1 week, depending on the weather and humidity in the kitchen. I also buy delicate dried rosebuds or dried marigolds, which can give a plate an unexpected herbal and floral flavor. I don't overdo it, just crushing a little in my hand and sprinkling it over the top. Look for dried flowers from spice companies, and always buy organic flowers. If they come from your mum's garden, that's even better.

TOOLS AND OTHER THINGS I LOVE

COCOTTE

A couple of years ago, I invested in a beautiful oval Staub cocotte (Dutch oven) that is large enough to fit a very big chicken; it's become one of the most beloved things in my kitchen. Not only is it beautiful, but it is also one of the most useful cooking vessels I have. In it, I braise beef, cook clams, and even form a nest of hay in it to cook Chicken in Hay (page 161), my tribute to the great chef Alain Passard. The most versatile size holds 7 quarts, which is big enough to braise a head of cabbage or cook a whole chicken. A cocotte can also be used for baking or braising in the oven, but since my oven is too tiny, I always use mine on the stove.

GRATERS AND GRINDERS

For grinding spices or making powder from dried herbs, I use a mortar and pestle, but feel free to use a spice grinder. I also keep a Microplane rasp on hand for grating citrus zest and a pepper mill to grind pepper when needed.

MIXERS / BLENDERS

I keep a hand-held electric mixer around for whipping cream and making meringue, as well as an immersion blender for making mayonnaise and smoothing out jam.

Pickles

Having pickles on hand is an easy way to add a bit of interest to what you're serving without too much extra effort. At La Buvette, I always have at least one type of seasonal pickle ready to serve with charcuterie, rotating the fruit or vegetable depending on what is in season. In the fall and winter, it's often pears, which I love to serve with terrine. In summer, the same plate might be decorated with bright pickled cherries. In the early days of the shop, I would buy pickles already made, drain off all the store-bought brine, and then soak them in homemade brine. It didn't take long to realize that it would be better to make the pickles from start to finish myself.

I use mild vinegars, such as cider vinegar, rice vinegar, or white balsamic vinegar, all of which blend easily with other flavors. If you are going to stock only one bottle of vinegar, however, rice vinegar is the best option—it is the most neutral and matches with nearly anything you would want to pickle. A brine can't be vinegar alone, so I dilute it with water and add a bit of sugar and salt to balance the flavors. I have experimented with pickling many different fruits and vegetables, and the following recipes represent some of my favorites. Making pickles is usually a forgiving project, as long as you avoid fresh mushrooms. I learned this lesson when I bought some beautiful, round special mushrooms, stuffed them in a jar, and poured in a hot brine. Imagine my disappointment when thirty minutes later I had found they had shrunk into tiny vinegar sponges, barely filling the jar.

The good thing about pickles is that you can reuse the brine to make a new batch, adding more vinegar and water to make up for lost volume. (The one big exception to this is brine from pickled eggs, (page 101, which takes on the aroma of sulfur and is best discarded). Some people make pickles to use months later, but I like serving pickles a day or two after making. Fresh pickles have a milder flavor, making them an easier match with wine. These recipes make small batches, but they can be increased if you have a lot of produce to preserve.

PEAR PICKLES

Slice the pears in half if they are baby pears or in quarters if they are larger. It is fine to leave the seeds and stem in place. Pack the pears snugly but gently into a quart jar or a heatproof storage container—whatever they will fit in comfortably.

In a pot, heat the vinegar, water, sugar, and salt together over medium heat until the sugar dissolves—it doesn't have to boil. Pour the brine over the pears and let the pickles cool on the counter. Once cool, cover and refrigerate for at least 1 day before eating. To me, pear pickles are best when used up within 1 week after making them, but they will keep for several weeks in the refrigerator, growing stronger in vinegar flavor.

MAKES 1 QUART

5 baby pears or 3 average-size pears (no more than 1¼ pounds total), preferably slightly underripe

1 cup cider vinegar

¾ cup water

3 tablespoons sugar

½ teaspoon fine sea salt

CHERRY PICKLES

When washing the cherries, take care to keep the stem intact (keeping the fruit whole, with stems in place, makes cherry pickles elegant to serve and prevents too much brine soaking in the fruit), and gently pack them into a pint jar or a heatproof storage container—whatever they will fit in comfortably without losing their stems.

In a pot, heat the vinegar, water, sugar, and salt together over medium heat until the sugar dissolves—it doesn't have to boil. Let the brine cool for a few minutes until it is the temperature of a hot bath. (The cherries are fragile, so it's better not to heat them too much.) Pour the brine over the cherries and let the pickles cool on the counter. Once cool, cover and refrigerate for at least 1 day before eating. The cherries are best within 1 week, but they will keep for several months in the refrigerator, growing stronger in vinegar flavor.

MAKES 1 PINT

8 ounces sweet cherries with their stems, preferably big and sweet but not overly ripe

⅔ cup rice vinegar

⅓ cup water

3 tablespoons sugar

1 teaspoon fine sea salt

½ teaspoon whole timut or sansho peppercorns*

*To accent the sweetness of the fruit, I infuse the brine with whole timut peppercorns, a beautiful citrus-like spice (that is actually not a true peppercorn). Japanese sansho peppercorns impart a similar flavor. If you can't find either, use good-quality black peppercorns.

BABY BEET PICKLES

Trim off the beet greens and the root end if it's very long, leaving about ½ inch of stem on each beet. Peel the beets (if using red beets, don a pair of gloves first if you want to avoid turning your hands pink for a couple of days). Cut any beets that are larger than the others in half or in quarters so the beet pieces will be about the same size and will cook evenly.

Bring a pot of water to a boil. Add the beets and cook until you can pierce them with the tip of a knife, but a fork will not go through the center, about 12 minutes. (You still want them to be a little firm). Drain and let cool.

When cool enough to handle, gently pack the beets into a quart or pint canning jar or a heatproof storage container—whatever they will fit in comfortably.

In a pot, heat the vinegar, water, sugar, and salt together over medium heat until the sugar dissolves. Pour the hot brine over the beets and let the pickles cool on the counter. Once cool, cover and refrigerate for at least 1 day before eating. Beet pickles keep for up to 6 months in the refrigerator.

MAKES 1 PINT

9 baby beets*, about 12 ounces (I use red, but other colors work, too)

1¼ cups white balsamic vinegar

¾ cup water

2 tablespoons sugar

¾ teaspoon fine sea salt

Feel free to use radishes in place of beets; just skip the beet-cooking step and pour the hot brine over the radishes.

BABY CARROT PICKLES

Trim off the greens, saving about ½ inch of stem on each carrot. Instead of peeling the carrots with a vegetable peeler, try scrubbing the carrots with a clean brush or sponge; the skin of baby carrots is thin enough that this is all you need to remove most of it. (You can also use a peeler, but be gentle so you remove only the skin, not the rest of the carrot.) You will have about 12 ounces of carrots once the greens and peels have been removed. Ensure that you scrape off any dirt around the base of the carrot stems with a paring knife.

Pack the carrots into a quart jar, or use a heatproof storage container that the carrots fit into comfortably.

In a pot, bring the vinegar, water, honey, and salt to a boil. (You want the brine to be really hot so its heat cooks the carrots, giving them the perfect consistency.) Pour the hot brine over the carrots and let the pickles cool on the counter. Once cool, cover and refrigerate for at least 1 day before eating. Carrot pickles keep for 6 months in the refrigerator.

MAKES 1 QUART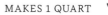

1 pound baby carrots*
(about 4 inches long and
no wider than 1 inch)

1¼ cups cider vinegar

¾ cup water

¼ cup honey

¾ teaspoon fine sea salt

If you are lucky enough to find baby carrots of different colors, don't hesitate in using them. The pickles look even nicer.

SPRING ONION JAM

When I was living on my own in my student apartment in
a suburb of Paris, I would go home from time to time on the
weekends to visit my family. On one of those visits, I was
flipping through my mum's copy of *Elle* magazine, which
for years included tear-out recipe cards printed on card
stock in the back of each issue. The issue was dedicated to
springtime, and on one of the cards was a recipe for this
chutney-style jam. I tore it out and stuck it in my recipe
notebook, making it a few weeks later while visiting friends
outside of Paris. They lived in a building with a shared
garden where we'd hang out with neighbors. Perfumed
with vanilla and candied orange, the jam was sweet but a
little savory, a perfect springtime condiment to serve with
cheese. It pairs well with everything from blue to Comté,
though my favorite to serve with this jam is goat cheese.

*Cut the onions into **quarters*** through the bulb end, but keep any onions
smaller than a marble whole. (I like to cut the onions in a way that
will help them hold their shape and not fall apart completely.) You
will have about 3 cups. Finely slice enough of the onion greens to
have 1 heaping cup and discard the remaining greens or save for
another use.

Combine the onions, candied orange peel, vanilla bean, cinnamon
stick, and saffron in a pot or saucepan (use what you will cook the jam
in). Stir in the salt and pepper. In a small bowl, whisk together the sugar
and pectin. Sprinkle the pectin sugar onto the onions and let macerate
for at least 30 minutes, or up to a couple of hours at room temperature.

CONTINUED

MAKES 2½ TO 3 CUPS

2 pounds white spring
onions*

½ cup finely diced candied
orange peel**

½ vanilla bean

1 cinnamon stick

A pinch of saffron (optional)

1¼ teaspoons fine sea salt

¼ teaspoon freshly ground
black pepper

¾ cup sugar

1½ tablespoons powdered
pectin

2 celery stalks, cut into small
cubes

*Look for spring onions with
round white bulbs in early to
mid spring. (Some markets
label them as "knob onions.")
Avoid spring onions with narrow red bulbs, which create a
different texture.*

**You can find candied orange
peel at specialty markets as
well as online.*

Put a plate in the refrigerator to chill. Put three 8-ounce jars in a pot large enough to hold them and cover with water. Bring the pot to a simmer over high heat, then turn the heat off and leave the jars in the water to keep them hot.

Stir the sugar into the onions and bring to a boil over high heat. Lower the heat to medium-high and cook until the juices begin to thicken and form large bubbles, about 8 minutes. At this point, dab a spoonful onto the chilled plate. If it stays in its place and doesn't run off when the plate is held at an angle, the jam is done. Turn off the heat and remove the vanilla bean and cinnamon stick. Stir in the celery.

Take the jars out of the water and place them on a kitchen towel. Spoon the jam into the jars and let cool to room temperature. Cap the jars, then store in the refrigerator. The jam can be eaten the day it's made or kept refrigerated for up to 4 months.

The first time I paid Julien Courtois a visit, I was a bit lost. It was also my first time visiting a winery, and I wasn't sure what to think when he showed me the soil in the vineyards or offered a taste of wine that was still aging in the barrel. Still, Julien was very patient, explaining what I needed to know in a discrete way. And even though it was only my first winemaker visit, I knew that I was in a remarkable place.

South of Orléans and surrounded by tributaries that feed into the Loire River, Sologne is an unlikely winemaking area in the Loire Valley. Instead of expansive stretches of vines found in Sancerre, it has woods and ponds, and it's here that the Courtois family has made wine for a few decades. Claude, the father, is a bit of a radical thinker and taught Julien and his brother, Etienne, the values in preserving the health of the soil in the vineyard as well as the importance of reviving old Loire Valley grapes that had been nearly forgotten. The three all work different parcels of land near each other, using many more grape varieties than is typical. And although Claude has handed off some of his vineyards to Etienne to manage, he still oversees a field blend of wine made of more than a dozen types of grapes grown in the same vineyard. This creation is his life's work and, fortunately, his sons are also making wine with similar passion.

When I opened La Buvette, I called Julien directly to say that I would be really happy to have his wines in my shop, and he was one of the first winemakers who agreed to let me stock their bottles. Over the years, some producers have cycled through the shop's inventory, but Julien's bottles will be there forever, not only because he is a friend but also because he makes exceptional wine. What I love most is that when I open a bottle from a new vintage, I can taste his signature at the first sip. It's a rare feeling, akin to hearing the first notes of music and knowing the composer. That's why I feel that his wines are very rare and beautiful. Julien's wife, Heidi Kuka, an artist from New Zealand, designs every label inspired by her Maori heritage. Every image on the labels—whether a butterfly, dragonfly, or beetle—relates to the living creatures on their land. Now that I'm not so shy around wineries, I try to pay Julien a visit every year to taste his wines, often making a day of it by bringing family and friends.

Dusts and Butters

I experiment with different dusts and butters at La Buvette all the time. My experiments can be as simple as crushing sheets of nori or dried herbs and mixing it into salted butter or as involved as dehydrating mandarin peels and blending them in a dust, but the idea is to make something new out of an everyday ingredient.

The idea behind making flavored butters came after tasting the butters of Jean-Yves Bordier, the legendary butter maker from Brittany. Bordier butters are made by hand, and they can be plain or flavored with anything from espelette pepper to *framboise* (raspberry). After doing my own experiments, I found that as long as I mixed butter with something perfectly dry (like one of my dusts), I could make a flavored butter. That discovery opened the door to my butter experiments. For this reason, the recipes in this book make small batches of butters to encourage experimenting. If you really love one of them, double the recipe, but keep in mind that the flavor becomes stronger the longer the butter sits in the refrigerator.

CONTINUED

DRIED MANDARIN PEELS OR DUST

The first time I bought Sicilian mandarins from Cédric of La Tête dans les Olives (see page 54), I loved them so much that I left the peels on the heater to perfume my flat with their intense aroma. In a couple of days, they were totally dehydrated, but instead of throwing them away, I decided to infuse the peels in cream for dessert, which worked well. Not long after, I was dusting raspberry powder over Burrata at La Buvette and started to wonder what the dried mandarin peels would taste like on this mild, creamy cheese. I ground the peels into a bright yellow-orange powder and used it to dust the cheese in place of the raspberry powder, and the pairing was so successful it became one of my classic dishes (page 97).

Now every winter I buy plenty of Cédric's mandarins for eating and for dehydrating the peels. I use most of the peels to make dust, but I also save a few to infuse into panna cotta (page 183), mulled wine (page 199), and even broth for cooking fish. Sometimes I also blend it with sugar for an orange-flavored sugar. Its versatility is one of the reasons it's become one of my favorite pantry ingredients.

Score the mandarins along the equator through the peel but not through the fruit. Using your fingers, pry the peel away from the flesh, keeping the peels in two half pieces. (If the peel is very thin and is sticking to the flesh, you may need to cut the fruit in quarters and use a knife to cut away the flesh.) With your fingers or a spoon, scrape away as much of the white pith as you can (if too much white pith is left, the dust will be bitter). Or cut the peel into quarters and use a knife pressed vertically against the peel to cut the pith away.

MAKES ABOUT ½ CUP

10 organic mandarins

Put the mandarins on a rimmed baking sheet and place in the oven. Turn the oven to 170°F and let the mandarins gently dry for 2 to 3 hours, until the peels are dry to the touch and firm in some places (they don't need to be completely dry). Turn the oven off and let the mandarins sit in the oven for another 2 to 3 hours, until the peels feel dry and firm and a bit leathery to the touch. The total amount of time will depend on the thickness of the mandarin peels and the humidity in the room. If the peels are still soft or tacky after 3 hours, turn the oven back to 170°F for another 30 minutes, then turn off the oven again and let them sit for another hour, or until they feel dry.

When completely dry, the peels can be stored in an airtight container in a cool area for up to 6 months. To grind the peels into dust, use a powerful blender, such as a Vitamix or Breville, and blend until a fine powder forms. If the peels are thin and break easily in your hands, you can also use a coffee grinder reserved for grinding spices, though this is not a good option for thicker peels (it may burn out the motor). Store mandarin peel dust in a tightly sealed glass jar in a cool area for up to 6 months. If the dust clumps up a bit because of humidity in the air, just crush it up in a mortar and pestle or with your hands. For a very "La Buvette" look, sift the dust through the finest mesh strainer you can find. This is what gives the dust a velvety effect on the plate.

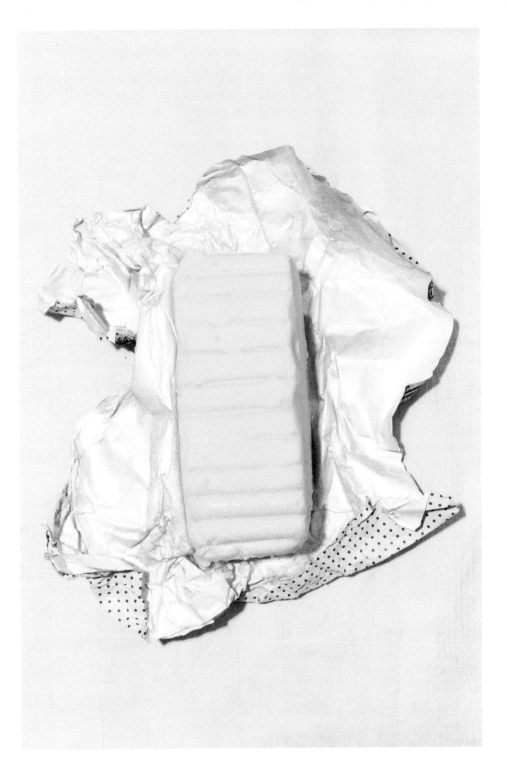

LA BUVETTE

SEAWEED BUTTER

Jean-Yves Bordier started mixing seaweed into butter years ago, creating an amazing salty, savory combination. Now that it is easy to find dehydrated seaweed in supermarkets, I started making my own version at home. The most available kind of seaweed is nori, but dehydrated wakame will work, too. If the seaweed is firm, grind it into a powder in a food processor or spice grinder. Otherwise, simply crush nori sheets with your hands or chop them with a knife into small flakes.

Combine the butter and nori in a bowl and mix it a bit with a spoon until the nori flakes are evenly distributed. Taste, adding the salt if desired (most nori and salted butter combinations are salty enough on their own). Shape the butter into a log on a piece of parchment paper and roll it up, twisting the ends snugly, to turn it into a shape that is easy for slicing. Seaweed butter keeps for about 2 weeks in the refrigerator.

Variation: In place of the seaweed, mix in 1 to 2 teaspoons of espelette pepper into the butter. I can't tolerate a lot of heat, but I know many love spicy food, and the espelette makes a colorful butter.

MAKES ½ CUP

½ cup salted butter, at room temperature

2 tablespoons crushed nori flakes

Sage Obsession

I started to become obsessed with sage a few years ago in New York while trying to come up with a new idea for a pop-up event. I have always liked the aroma of sage and had recently discovered sage sticks used for incense. This wasn't like the sage I knew at all. I started wondering how to capture the aroma of its smoke in food without doing any cooking. Because dairy fat captures flavor easily, my first idea was to infuse sage smoke into some type of dairy, but I wasn't sure if it would work. Later that day, I was walking around the city when I saw burnt sage ice cream on the menu at Morgenstern's Finest Ice Cream. At the time, I remember feeling a little heartbroken that someone had this idea before me, but I was not brokenhearted enough to resist ordering a scoop. The flavors worked so well that I knew I needed to make my own thing with smoked sage. And this is how Burnt Sage Butter (page 74) came to be.

My obsession with sage goes further than this story. I also like making a dust out of dried sage, which I use not only to flavor butter but also to sprinkle on top of dessert. If you happen to have dried fig leaves or dried nettle leaves, you can use those dusts to make butters as well.

CONTINUED

SAGE DUST

Bundle the sage up with a rubber band and hang it in the kitchen until it dries, about 4 days, depending on the humidity in the air. Once dried, pull off the tough stems and grind the leaves into a fine dust in a mortar and pestle or in a spice grinder.

MAKES ABOUT ½ CUP

1 bunch sage

SAGE BUTTER

Put the butter, sage dust, and salt in a bowl and mix it a bit with a spoon until the flecks of sage are evenly distributed. Shape the butter into a log on a piece of parchment paper and roll it up, twisting the ends snugly, to turn it into a shape that is easy for slicing. Don't be disappointed if the butter is not tasty enough at first, because the taste will become stronger within a couple of days. Refrigerate at least 1 day before using. Sage butter keeps for about 2 weeks in the refrigerator.

MAKES ½ CUP

½ cup salted butter, at room temperature

1 tablespoon Sage Dust (see recipe above)

Pinch of flaky sea salt, such as Maldon

BURNT SAGE BUTTER

Put the butter in a fine-mesh strainer.

Light the incense stick. Hold the strainer in one hand, while in the other hand, hold the incense stick under the strainer so the smoke plume goes into the butter. Smoke the butter for 3 minutes and taste it; it should taste smoky. If you want a stronger smoke flavor, do it for 1 minute more.

Put the butter in a bowl and mix it a bit with a spoon (you don't need to stir it much if it has started to soften). Shape the butter into a log on a piece of parchment paper as best you can if the butter is still a bit chilled and roll it up, twisting the ends snugly, to turn it into a shape that is easy for slicing. Burnt sage butter keeps for about 2 weeks in the refrigerator.

MAKES ½ CUP

½ cup salted butter, cold enough to hold its shape, cubed

1 sage incense stick*

A sage incense stick (also called a sage incense roll or sage smudge stick) is made up of a bunch of dried sage sprigs tied tightly together. Look for it in homeopathic stores or places that sell incense. Make sure to burn the sage in a well-ventilated room with an open window; the smoke can be strong.

HOW THE *CAVE À MANGER* CAME TO BE

The phrase *cave à manger*, a wine shop for eating, is probably no more than a couple of decades old. Even so, it would be hard to imagine Paris without these establishments. In 2012 when I opened La Buvette, there were already a few *caves* serving food, and there are plenty more today. The rise of caves à manger also reflects the popularity of natural wine and the community that has grown around it. But a main reason that there are so many *caves* with food in Paris today has to do with practicality. To pour a taste of wine for customers in my shop, I have to follow the requirements of my alcohol license, which allows me to serve wine for customers only if they order something to eat. I benefit by giving my customers a taste of a wine they may have never tried, and they benefit because they can drink and eat in a casual, fun environment.

Still, I am not the first to embrace the charms of a cave à manger. In French, we say *"il faut rendre à César ce qui est à César,"* ("you must return to Caesar what is Caesar's"), which means to give credit where credit is due. Many wine professionals before me created the foundation for what makes Paris such a fun place to drink natural wine today.

***

In 1987 when Tim Johnston opened Juveniles, his 2ème wine shop and bar, he tried serving a tapas-style menu with a selection of the Rhône wines he was crazy about. But in those years, Parisians always asked what else was on the menu—no one wanted to go to a place just for wine and small plates of food. So he evolved, expanding the menu to more of a bistro style and bringing in different wines. Today, Juveniles is still a *cave*, but it is also a cozy bistro owned by Romain Roudeau in the kitchen and Tim's daughter Margaux Johnston in the dining room. Tim jokes that Margaux took her first order at Juveniles when she

(from left) Margaux Johnston, Tim Johnston, and Romain Roudeau

Nadine Decailly

continued from page 75

was four years old, but Margaux insists that her father is exaggerating, though she has long been an integral part of Juveniles.

Because Tim is Scottish, Romain stocks beautiful cheeses from Neal's Yard Dairy, and he even kept haggis on the menu for the longest time. Otherwise, everything else is French. In 1987, Juveniles may have been one of the first to try creating a cave à manger style of place in Paris, but Paris wasn't ready for it in those days, so Tim adapted.

That slowly started to change in the 1990s. Nadine Decailly, a Parisian typographer, liked to visit a tiny restaurant in the 14ème on Thursday nights. The kitchen would close for the evening and people would come in to drink cheap Beaujolais, eat charcuterie and cheese, and sing old-fashioned French songs. "It was a great kind of atmosphere, the kind of place you want to go and stay for a while," Nadine recalls. Even though the wine and food weren't all that memorable, the idea of sharing a moment with others started to change the way Nadine felt about wine and what she wanted to do with her life.

While Nadine was singing French songs in the 14ème, a group of friends were also thinking about how to drink good wine and hang out in a more casual, direct way. Cyril Bordarier, Olivier Labarde, and Jean-Michel Wilmes worked together at Le Repaire de Bacchus, a chain of wine shops. The particular location where they worked also served charcuterie, allowing customers to hang out a little longer. "We thought this was so cool," Cyril says. "The day we had our own businesses, we all wanted to do the same thing."

Eating in a wine shop was one idea. The other idea—the conviction that the wine served should be made in a clean, conscientious way that we now call natural—came a little later. While the friends sold conventional wines at Le Repaire de Bacchus, Olivier introduced them to wines made with organic grapes and natural processes in the cellar. Through *bouche à oreille* (word of mouth), the friends started to ask around looking for more places to drink this kind of wine. They ended up hanging out with Rodolphe Paquin, the chef of Le Repaire de Cartouche, and the owners of Le Baratin, a bistro in Belleville at La Cave du Square Trousseau next to the Marché d'Aligre. It was one of the few places in Paris to drink natural wines.

Other bistros also started quietly building wine collections in this new style. Chef Christian Maurel, who runs Le Bougainville in Galerie Vivienne with his wife, Michelle, and daughter, Carole, discretely began pouring more natural wines.

The friends soon moved on from the conventional wine shop to take their interest in natural wine more seriously. In 1998, Jean-Michel opened Aux Crieurs de Vin (meaning the "town crier of wine") in Troyes, a city in the southern part of the Champagne region. Today the *bar à vins* (wine bar) and restaurant, which Jean-Michel runs with Franck Windel, has become a favorite place in the Aube for natural wine. The same year, Olivier opened La Part des Anges in Nice, naming his *cave* after the French phrase that describes the wine that evaporates from the barrel, the portion that the angels drink. By the late 1990s, Nadine had left Paris and her career as a typographer to study to become a sommelier in Nice. There, she discovered Olivier's place, which looked like a regular wine shop from the street but served cold food and wine by the glass in the evenings.

Cyril Bordarier

One night Nadine tried her first natural wine, Nuit d'Ivresse (Tipsy Night), a Cabernet Franc from the Loire Valley made by Catherine and Pierre Breton. "After I tasted this new type of wine without all the complexity that was added to wine for no good reason, that's all I wanted to drink," she says. Soon she was spending as much time as she could at Olivier's shop, doing a *stage* there a couple of nights a week after sommelier classes.

During this time, Cyril prepared to open his own *cave* in Paris. To research the wines he wanted to stock, he drove around France visiting winemakers who were making this natural style of wine. He spent time in the Loire Valley and also got to know the Laurent family behind Domaine Gramenon, which today is one of his most important producers. In 2000, he opened Le Verre Volé (which means "the stolen glass") next to the Canal Saint-Martin with fifty wines and a very simple menu. He had created a cave à manger, but he didn't call it that yet.

It was a loud, small place, with a tiny window for a kitchen where Cyril would cook *caillette* (meatballs wrapped in caul fat) in a broiler and serve cheese and slices of terrine. Caillette became so emblematic of Cyril that they called him Cyril Caillette. (When I first heard about him, I thought his name really was Cyril Caillette!) Most people didn't come specifically for natural wine, which no one really knew much about. Instead, his friends came to party, and old-fashioned wine industry professionals came to laugh at what he was doing. But word began to spread among restaurant insiders about this place that was pouring cuvées for people ready to have an adventure with wine. By 2001, the influential publication *Le Fooding* named Le Verre Volé the best cave à manger in Paris. That made it official: Le Verre Volé and other places like it weren't *bars à vins* or *caves* or bistros or restaurants. They were caves à manger—wine shops for eating.

After working abroad, Nadine returned to Paris with the intention of opening a cave à manger with a focus on natural wine. At the time, some organic grocery stores sold wines that were labeled "organic," but most of it was just old hippie wine, with no technique behind it. Because these terrible bottles were associated with natural wines, no one wanted to drink anything called "natural." Nadine knew that the best way to change people's minds was to have them taste it, so the cave à manger idea was perfect for her. In 2003, Nadine opened Au Nouveau Nez, a compact 250-square-foot cave à manger in the 11ème, not too far from where I would later open La Buvette. The name was a play on the French word for a newborn baby (*nouveau né*), because she thought you should approach drinking natural wines with newborn nose, one that was willing to experience a purer, cleaner kind of wine. She had an inventory of 100 to 150 bottles, all of which she knew intimately, and people stood at the counter eating charcuterie, *saucisson*, and cheese—anything that was easy but good.

Today, there are places that call themselves caves à manger all over the city. Some have full kitchens and feel much more like restaurants and some are tiny spots. In 2010, Cyril expanded his space and built a proper kitchen. You can now get a reservation for a table, just like a regular restaurant. But some things stay the same. The wines are written on a chalkboard, and it may just say *pét-nat* (naturally sparkling wine) and you get whatever they're pouring that day. Still, you know it's going to be good. It's this vision of creating spaces for drinking good wine in a casual way that set the foundation for my generation of *cavistes* to succeed.

(from left) Carole, Michelle, and Christian Maurel

AT LA BUVETTE

These are the kinds of dishes that make up my repertoire at La Buvette, the perfect foods to serve when you don't want to be trapped in the kitchen. Some of what you'll find here aren't really true recipes at all but rather suggestions for dishes that are easy to prepare and serve. For this reason, I give suggested quantities instead of exact measurements to emphasize flexibility and ease. Other recipes do require cooking, but they can be made ahead. Which is what makes these kinds of dishes the perfect thing to serve when all you want to do is chat with friends and drink wine.

"FAMOUS" GIANT BEANS AND CITRUS ZEST

One of my earliest ideas for the menu at La Buvette came from opening a can of cooked *judión* beans—giant white beans imported from Spain—and seasoning them with a bit of olive oil, Maldon salt, and bergamot zest. I never anticipated that these beans would turn into something that people would come from all over the planet to eat. The key to this very simple dish is the fresh citrus grated on top, which brightens up the flavor of the beans. I change the citrus from bergamot to mandarin to lemon or citron— whatever looks most appealing for the season. In the spring when foraging season begins, I sometimes decorate the beans with edible flowers, such as chive flowers or garlic flowers. But I don't dare change much else, and I can never take them off the menu (I tried once and everyone kept asking, "Where are the beans?"). Today, I suppose that *gros haricots blancs & zeste de citron* have become La Buvette's "famous" beans, but I say it with a wink—can beans from a can truly be famous?

Spoon the beans into a bowl or plate. Drizzle with olive oil until the beans look shiny. Add a good pinch of salt and grate zest directly over the top to finish.

SERVES 2 TO 4

1 (14- to 15-ounce) can or jar of high-quality giant white beans, rinsed well and drained*

Extra-virgin olive oil, for drizzling

Flaky sea salt, such as Maldon, for seasoning

1 lemon or other type of citrus fruit, for grating

The beans I use come ready to eat. Look for cans or jars of plump judión, *gigante, corona, or any large, tender beans you can find. Before using, rinse them well. Depending on what else is on the table, plan on ½ to 1 cup of beans per person.*

"I don't like Cabernet Franc." "I don't drink Beaujolais." I've heard these phrases from people countless times over the years. These days, I have also seen a new generation of wine lovers who fall into the habit of drinking only the same favorite wines, afraid to try something new. In all of these cases, I'd like to suggest becoming a little more open-minded about what you drink.

For instance, Alsace is a small area and grows Muscat, Gewürztraminer, and other grapes that have a reputation for being too exuberant or making only sweet wine. Yet these wines can be quite delicious in the right hands. This is why I pour wines from places like Alsace: I want to help my customers think differently about wines that can be overlooked. The wines I select at the shop may be more on the edge of what people expect a specific grape or wine from a particular area tastes like. By pouring the wines I do, I challenge my customers to reconsider their expectations.

If you say to me you don't like wines from Alsace, for example, I may pour Zegwur, an Alsatian wine made by Yann Durrman. It is a simple, naked wine that is very pure and juicy. It has an exuberant smell, almost like a flower bouquet, which at first feels like too much. But when you taste it, it changes into something light and fresh and very grapey. The difference between the nose and the taste is something you wouldn't expect, and it would be a shame to miss it all because of a misconception. If you can stay a bit more curious about wine, it will keep you open to new experiences. So when customers tell me they don't like a specific kind of wine, I jokingly say to them, "Just taste it. If you don't like it, I will drink it." It's a little trick I use that works nearly every time.

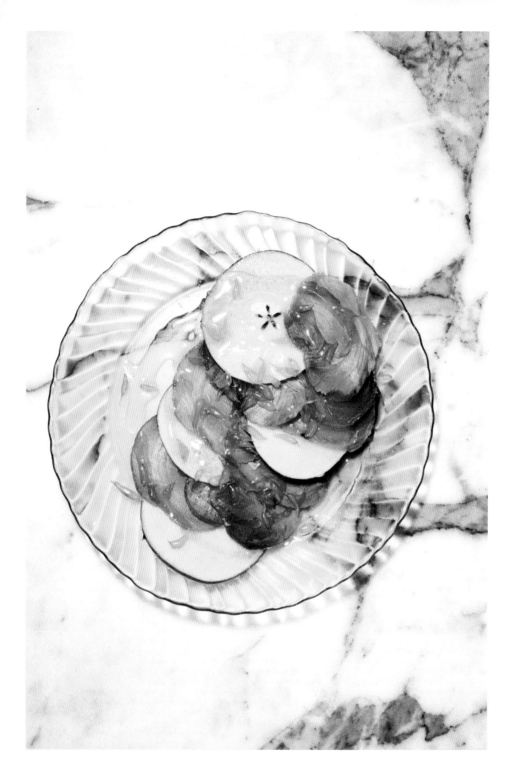

LA BUVETTE

SMOKED FISH, SLICED PEARS, AND POMELO PULP

A few years ago, I found this incredible smoked tuna cured in a way that made it taste and look more like charcuterie than fish. The salty, smoky flavor makes it such a perfect snack to have with wine that I've been serving it ever since. One day, my friend Alix Lacloche (the inspiration behind the pizzettes recipe, page 153) stopped by the shop with a box of finger limes. In French, they are called citrus caviar for two reasons: the texture of the pulp resembles caviar and they are expensive and hard to find. I loved the presentation of the pulp on cured fish, so I started to look for another way to get a similar effect. This is what led me to pomelo: the large, round citrus sold in Paris at Asian markets has a tart, juicy pulp that pops in your mouth.

If the fish feels wet after taking it out of the package, pat it dry. If using scallops, slice them in thirds. If using trout, break up the fillets into bite-sized pieces. Slice the pear thinly crosswise from the stem end to the bottom so it forms rounds (it's perfectly fine to see some of the seeds, though you can pick them out). Make alternating layers of the fish and pear slices across a plate resembling scales of a fish. Drizzle olive oil on top and season with a pinch of salt, depending on how salty the fish is.

Using your fingers, peel away the pith and membrane from the pomelo segments and separate the pulp into smaller pieces. Scatter the pulp over the pears and fish to finish.

SERVES 2 TO 4

3 to 4 ounces smoked and cured fish or seafood, such as trout, scallops, or tuna*

1 small, crisp (not-too-ripe) pear

Extra-virgin olive oil, for drizzling

Flaky sea salt, such as Maldon, for seasoning (optional)

3 pomelo segments

The smoked tuna I buy isn't the easiest type of smoked fish to find. Smoked trout and smoked scallops work just as well. It is best to have smoked fish that is a bit firm. Smoked and cured salmon tends to be too soft for this preparation.

LA BUVETTE

CHEESE   When I was a kid, a truck stopped by my grandparents'
house twice a week selling cheeses wrapped in paper
printed with a map of the origin of each French cheese.
Even though there were other options to choose from in
the truck, my grandfather always bought the same thing:
a well-aged Brie, and I remember becoming obsessed with
the wrapping paper, studying it to learn where all of my
favorite cheeses came from.

For my grandfather, a meal without cheese was like a day
without sun, and while I inherited by grandfather's love of
cheese, I am not quite as nationalistic about it. I love Burrata
from Puglia, and any time I visit London, I try to find time
to visit Neal's Yard Dairy, a shop that posts signs about
cheeses with a crazy amount of detail, almost down to the
name of the cow that was milked to make it. But, of course,
I still love the cheeses of France. A few years ago, I found
an old-fashioned cheese shop near my apartment that
wrapped cheese in the same cheese-map paper I knew as
a kid, and I was filled with nostalgia.

At La Buvette, my friend Kamel Tabti picks out selections
from the Rungis wholesale market (see page 125), where
everything from huge wheels of Comté to delicate goat
cheeses stacked in wooden crates line an entire pavilion
of cheese. Twice a week, he texts me with what he has and
I place my order. I love serving a raw-milk Brillat Savarin
or a classic triple-crème cheese, and I also often get a nice
blue cheese for something a little stronger in flavor. No
matter the cheese, I always serve it at room temperature to
taste the flavor and texture in an optimal way. To me, it is
also better to serve one really good cheese than a variety
of cheeses that vary in quality, and for that I may have my
grandfather and his love of Brie to thank.

WINE AND CHEESE

Why do so many people consider red wine the best to drink with cheese? This is something I always heard, even at my grandfather's table. When I started learning about wine, it was one of my first questions, and even today I feel that there are many more options for cheese pairings with white wine. I prefer whites that are rich, rounded, and deep to pair with cheese. With red wine, you have more structure and tannin, and sometimes the tannins can fight with the flavor and texture of fermented milk. To me, a pairing should not be a fight. It should be like a couple dancing cheek to cheek. And while there are exceptions to this rule, this kind of happy pairing is easier to achieve with white wine and cheese than with red. Try it for yourself by tasting a favorite cheese with a couple of white wines.

LA BUVETTE

BURRATA AND MANDARIN PEEL DUST

Years ago, I sampled a very good Burrata from Puglia and liked it so much that I had to add it to my menu. A good Burrata tastes mild and creamy, which makes it easy to pair with a range of flavors, from raspberry powder to matcha, which Danny Bowien tried once during pop-up that we did together at Mission Chinese in New York. But my most typical way of serving Burrata is this version with mandarin peel dust, a dish that has become a classic at the shop.

Take the cheese out of the refrigerator at least 20 minutes before serving so it is at room temperature. Blot the Burrata dry with a paper towel and place it on a small plate or in a bowl. Drizzle the cheese with olive oil and season with salt. Position a small fine-mesh strainer above the Burrata and sift the dust over the top until it evenly coats the cheese (you may only need half of the tablespoon).

SERVES 2

1 large ball Burrata*

Extra virgin olive oil, for drizzling

Flaky sea salt, such as Maldon, for seasoning

1 tablespoon Mandarin Peel Dust (page 68)

*Look for creamy, fresh Burrata. It doesn't have to come from Puglia; freshly made Burrata is much better than Burrata that spent days in transport. If good Burrata is hard to find, use good mozzarella. Estimate 1 ball of Burrata for two people—or one person, if it's a hungry crowd.

GOAT CHEESE, BLACK GARLIC, AND CHERRIES

Sisters Tatiana and Katia Levha have two amazing restaurants down the street from La Buvette: Le Servan, a bistro that blends their French and Filipino backgrounds on the menu, and Double Dragon, which has an Asian menu served with a casual, cantine spirit. Katia runs the front of the restaurants while Tatiana is the chef, creating menus that always introduce me to new ideas. On one of my visits to Le Servan, I learned that Tatiana makes her own black garlic by fermenting it in a rice cooker for a couple of weeks. One day I will try the technique, but for now I buy black garlic. One of the reasons that chefs like Tatiana love black garlic is because it tastes sweet but not sugary, almost like an aged balsamic vinegar. That's why I love it with goat cheese and cherries, it becomes the perfect balance between sweetness and something more complex.

Using your fingers, smear the black garlic onto the base of a small plate to create a thin layer. Put the goat cheese on top, squashing it a bit with a spoon so it's broken up. Drizzle with olive oil and add a good pinch of salt. Top with hazelnuts and cherries.

SERVES 2

2 or 3 black garlic cloves*

2 ounces fresh goat cheese

Extra-virgin olive oil, for drizzling

Flaky sea salt, such as Maldon, for seasoning

A spoonful of crushed toasted hazelnuts

4 to 5 fresh cherries, halved and pitted, or a mix of fresh cherries and Cherry Pickles (page 59)

*Look for black garlic next to the seasonings and spices at a specialty foods store (it is not usually sold next to regular garlic in the produce section).

PICKLED EGGS AND FURIKAKE

In Andrew Tarlow's *Dinner at the Long Table*, a book I love, almost every recipe inspires me to want to spend a weekend in the countryside cooking with friends. By going from page to page, I found the simplest recipe to make: pickled eggs turned pink with beets. That night I made the eggs. And then the next day I loved them so much that I made them again, playing around with the brine and the toppings to make it my own. I was immediately in love with this recipe.

I still make it often, modifying the original to fit my mood. While I keep the pickling base the same, I am flexible with the toppings. After my first trip to Japan, I became even more experimental, sprinkling toasted sesame seeds or puffed rice on top of the eggs, and that is only a start. For this recipe, I also encourage you to rely on your own creativity for toppings.

In a pot, combine 1 cup of the vinegar with the water, sugar, and fine sea salt and bring to a boil. Let cool to room temperature. (Alternatively, feel free to recycle some of the brine from Baby Carrot Pickles, page 62, or Baby Beet Pickles, page 61. Never reuse the brine you pickle the eggs in because the eggs impart a sulfur smell.)

Fill a separate pot with water and bring to boil with the remaining 1 tablespoon vinegar. Once the water boils, gently lower the eggs into the water and cook them for 8 minutes if the eggs start out at room temperature, or 9 minutes if the eggs are cold. While the eggs cook, set up a bowl of ice water to put the eggs in once they're finished cooking. Remove the eggs, submerge them in the ice water, and let them cool completely, about 10 minutes.

Peel the eggs and put them in a quart jar or a storage container that the eggs fit into comfortably. Pour the brine on top, then cover and refrigerate for at least 1 day before serving.

To serve, slice the eggs in half and season with a pinch of flaky sea salt. Sprinkle furikake or a topping of your choice on top to finish. The eggs will keep in the brine in the refrigerator for up to 1 week.

SERVES 4 TO 6

1 cup rice vinegar, plus 1 tablespoon for cooking the eggs

½ cup water

2 tablespoons sugar

1 teaspoon fine sea salt

6 eggs*

Flaky sea salt, such as Maldon, for seasoning

A few pinches of furikake**

It's best not to use the freshest eggs from the market, since fresh eggs tend to stick to the shell when you're trying to peel them. When you visit an Asian market, look for a Chinese spider skimmer, which will make it easier to lower the eggs into and out of the hot water all at once.

**Buy a furikake mix at a Japanese grocery store or make your own out of nori, toasted sesame seeds, and puffed rice. Wasabi- or yuzu-roasted sesame seeds are also fun to mix in, if you can find them. Or roll the eggs in crushed black sesame seeds before cutting them in half for a dramatic appearance. If other ingredients are out of reach, crush a sheet of nori over the eggs instead.*

EGG + EGGS

Two classic ways to serve eggs in Paris bistros is *œufs mimosa*—which is close to what Americans call "deviled eggs" except that some of the grated hard-boiled yolk is sprinkled on top—and *œufs mayo*, where hard-boiled eggs are sliced in half and then coated on top with mayonnaise. This is my version of *œufs mayo* in which I decorate the egg halves with a spoonful of salmon roe so it becomes egg *with eggs*. I love how salmon roe pops in the mouth, giving each bite a little texture and saltiness.

My biggest problem when trying to create this recipe is that I am bad at making mayonnaise. Chris Wilson, who, with his wife Christine, owns Broken Biscuits, a charming Anglo-French *pâtisserie* near La Buvette, helped me figure out how to make infallible mayonnaise: use a whole egg (not just the yolk) and blend it with an immersion blender.

To make the eggs, fill a pot with water and bring to a boil with the vinegar. Once the water boils, gently lower the eggs into the water and cook them for 8 minutes, if the eggs are at room temperature, or for 9 minutes, if the eggs are cold. While the eggs cook, set up a bowl of ice water. Remove the eggs when done, submerge them in the ice water, and let them cool completely, about 10 minutes. Once cool, drain and peel the eggs.

To make the mayonnaise, combine the egg, water, vinegar, mustard, and salt in a bowl and blend a few times with the immersion blender. While blending, slowly drizzle in the oil, starting with a few drops and then forming a thin stream, until the ingredients form an emulsion and look like mayonnaise. Taste and add a little more salt, if desired. You can use the mayonnaise immediately or refrigerate it in a sealed container for a few days. You will have about 1½ cups.

To serve, cut the eggs in half and season the yolks with a pinch of sea salt. Spoon a little mayonnaise on top of each half and then spoon the salmon roe on top. Garnish with flowers.

SERVES 6

Eggs

1 tablespoon cider vinegar or red wine vinegar

6 eggs

Flaky sea salt, such as Maldon, for seasoning

A handful of chive flowers or leaves, such as peppery watercress

1 small jar (about 3 ounces) salmon roe or other large fish roe

Mayonnaise

1 egg, at room temperature

1 tablespoon water, at room temperature

1 tablespoon cider vinegar or red wine vinegar

1 heaping tablespoon Dijon mustard (the smooth kind), at room temperature

¼ teaspoon fine sea salt, plus more if needed

1 cup sunflower or other neutral vegetable oil

CURED DUCK MAGRET

After one of her neighbors started to bring my mum these beautiful, fat duck breasts—*magret*—from the southwest of France, she started experimenting with preserving them in salt. My grandfather used to make his own brandy, and let's just say that it was better not to drink it. Instead, my mum used it to "disinfect" the duck meat after it was cured by pouring a little brandy on top. (In reality, this is less about cleanliness than it is about flavor, and it is an optional step.) Inspired by my mum's successes, I started to cure duck *magret*, too, finding it is actually a very simple thing to make in my home refrigerator. Plan to make it 3 weeks in advance. I like to serve the meat sliced alongside one of my sage butters for *apéro* (see pages 202–203).

Put 2 cups of the salt in a container that will fit the duck (try a loaf pan for one breast or an 8-inch square pan for 2 breasts). Place the duck on top, then pour the rest of the salt over the duck so it is completely covered. Refrigerate and let the meat cure for 12 hours.

Pull the duck out of the salt and wipe off the excess. Discard the salt. Season the duck with the pepper and then wrap in a clean, dry kitchen towel (avoid terrycloth towels; thin towels work better). Put the wrapped duck on a plate and place on the top shelf of the refrigerator. Let it cure until firm and dry to the touch, 2 to 3 weeks. (I wait until the duck is completely dark on the outside but still a little pink in the center. If you wait too long, the breast will be the same color all the way through and turns into jerky.) When ready, it should give slightly when pressed.

To serve, slice the breast crosswise. (It is easier to slice when cold, but it is better to eat when at room temperature.) Keep any unsliced duck tightly wrapped in parchment paper in the refrigerator so it can breathe. The cured breast keeps for up to 1 month, but it will continue to dry out the longer you keep it. Since I like it tender, I prefer to eat it within 1 week.

SERVES ABOUT 6

3 cups kosher salt or coarse gray sea salt

1 large duck breast (about 12 ounces)*

1 teaspoon freshly ground black pepper**

The duck magret *in France is larger than most of the duck breasts sold in the United States. You can also use 2 smaller breasts about 5 to 6 ounces each. Smaller duck breasts may be perfectly cured in 2 weeks, so it's best to follow the texture descriptions in the recipe to know when it's ready.*

**For an alternative version, mix crushed Sichuan peppercorns in place of some of the black pepper.*

RILLETTES

At 4 or 5 a.m., butchers at Rungis, the famous wholesale market outside of Paris (page 125), pack into Le Saint Hubert, their local café for rillettes sandwiches. Made by cooking meat in its own fat and then mixing it until soft enough to spread on bread, rillettes are a delicious but simple food. This recipe is adapted from *Terrines* by Rodolphe Paquin, the chef and owner of Le Repaire de Cartouche in Paris. It is not hard to make rillettes, but it does take time. This recipe makes a large quantity, but extra keeps for a while in the refrigerator since a layer of fat on the surface of the meat helps preserve it. If you have rillettes and cornichons, you have the perfect combination, if not for early-morning sandwiches then for *apéro* with a glass of easy-to-drink wine.

In a 7-quart cocotte or Dutch oven, mix together the pork shoulder, pork belly, lard, water, wine, and garlic. Put the thyme and bay leaves on top. Bring the pot to a simmer over medium-high heat, then lower the heat to as low as the flame will go, cover, and cook until the meat is completely tender and easy to pull apart when pierced with a fork, 2½ to 3 hours. Stir occasionally to prevent scorching on the bottom and to ensure that the meat stays submerged in liquid and fat.

Remove the herbs. Using a spider skimmer or large slotted spoon, transfer the meat into a large bowl.

Bring the cooking juices to a simmer over medium heat and cook to reduce the juices and concentrate the flavors, about 10 minutes. Turn off the heat and let it sit for 5 to 10 minutes to cool slightly. Strain the liquid to get rid of any solids, then stir in the vinegar. (If you add the vinegar when the juices are hot, it can splatter and make a mess if most of the water has evaporated from the liquid.) You will have 3 to 4 cups of liquid, most of which is fat.

CONTINUED

SERVES 12 OR MORE
(MAKES 6 CUPS)

1½ pounds boneless pork shoulder, cut into 1-inch cubes

1½ pounds skinless pork belly, cut into 1-inch cubes

8 ounces rendered lard*

¾ cup water

¾ cup white wine

1 large garlic clove, peeled but left whole

5 thyme sprigs

3 bay leaves

½ cup cider vinegar

1 tablespoon fine sea salt

1 teaspoon freshly ground black pepper

Look for lard at well-stocked butcher shops. The best kind comes from butcher shops that make their own.

When the meat is cool enough to handle, shred it into small pieces using your hands or a pair of forks. Add the salt and pepper and taste the meat, keeping in mind that the rillettes will be served cold, so it should taste slightly salty at this point. Add more salt, if desired.

Stir the liquid into the shredded meat ½ cup at a time until the shredded meat looks generously coated and glossy. You may need only 1 cup. Pack the rillettes into small glass jars or one large container, then pour about ¼ inch of extra liquid on top to seal it from the air. Refrigerate for 24 hours before serving. Rillettes will keep for about 2 weeks in the refrigerator.

LA BUVETTE TERRINE

Inside Galerie Vivienne, a historic building just north of
Le Palais Royal, the bistro Le Bougainville looks the same
as it did years ago, with gold columns, red vinyl seats, and a
Formica bar. Maybe that's part of its charm. Chef Christian
Maurel also has a very good wine collection, and I like to
stop by and pay a visit to his daughter, Carole. She grew up
working in restaurants in Paris and still remembers when
her grandparents ran Le Bougainville and let their dog wan-
der all over the dining room. I have always loved the bistro's
terrine de campagne (country terrine), which is filled with
dried apricots, pistachios, and chicken livers, so years ago I
had it in my mind to serve something similar at La Buvette.

It took me a while to get comfortable making terrines, but it
has given me a lot of pleasure to experiment with different
variations to get the results I had in mind. And there are few
things more satisfying to serve friends than a terrine you've
made yourself. While you can eat it the day after it's made,
it's best after aging in the refrigerator for a week.

In a large bowl, mix the chicken livers, pork shoulder, backfat, Cognac,
salt, black pepper, and espelette pepper. Cover and refrigerate for
12 to 24 hours.

Preheat the oven to 375°F. Have a baking pan and a 9 by 5-inch loaf
pan or terrine mold ready (ceramic or glass preferably over metal). Set
up a meat grinder for a medium grind and have a large bowl ready to
catch the ground meat. (If your grinder comes with only a small and a
large-sized grind setting, use the large size.)

CONTINUED

MAKES ONE 2½-POUND
TERRINE, SERVES 10

12 ounces chicken livers, cut
in half *See note on page 108

1 pound boneless pork
shoulder, cut into ½-inch
cubes

8 ounces skinless pork
fatback, cut into ½-inch
cubes**

3 tablespoons Cognac or
Armagnac

1 tablespoon fine sea salt

1 teaspoon freshly ground
black pepper

¼ teaspoon espelette pepper

⅔ cup heavy cream

10 dried apricots, cut into
pieces with scissors to the
same size as pistachios

¼ cup shelled pistachios

Remove the livers from the marinated meat. Grind three-quarters of the livers into the bowl, then grind the shoulder meat and fat. (If you want to "clean" your grinder, grind a piece of bread through it to dislodge any bits of meat. The bread can be mixed into the terrine if you'd like.)

Stir the remaining livers into the ground meat along with the cream, apricots, and pistachios. The mixture will look a bit pink, but that's perfectly fine.

Put the mixture in the loaf pan, smoothing the top with a spatula, and cover with aluminum foil. Put the loaf pan in the baking pan and pour enough hot water into the baking pan so it comes halfway up the sides of the loaf pan. Bake for 35 minutes, then remove the foil. Bake for 35 more minutes, or until a knife inserted into the center of the terrine comes out releasing clear juices.

Let cool to room temperature, then cover with plastic wrap and refrigerate overnight. The terrine is best a week after making it and keeps in the refrigerator for a couple of weeks.

*If you love the taste of livers like I do, leave ½ to ¾ of the livers whole for a stronger flavor.

**Call your butcher shop ahead for fatback to ensure they carry it before you start. Butchers that make their own sausages often have fatback on hand, even if they don't have it on display.

***If you don't have a meat grinder, you can chop the meat by hand to make the terrine. After marinating the meat, remove the livers and line a tray with plastic wrap. Lay the marinated meat and fat on top in one layer. Cover with another sheet of plastic wrap and place in the freezer until the meat is firm to touch, about 1 hour. Once firm, chop the meat into pieces no larger than a pistachio. Chop half of the livers finely and then mix everything in a bowl and mix in the rest of the livers, cream, apricots, and pistachios and proceed with the recipe. The result will be a bit more rustic, but the results will be equally as tasty.

Several years ago, Ivo Ferreira, who makes wine in the southern Languedoc region, offered me a taste of La Petite Pépée, a white wine made with red grapes. The story goes that Ivo had it in his mind to make a white wine that would be much dryer, fresher, and straighter than the typical white wines made in the Languedoc, which is a warm region in the South of France. So he harvested Grenache Noir very early to preserve the red grapes' acidity and then made the wine as if the grapes were white, skipping skin contact. After I tasted it, he told me he had made only a few bottles. I thought, "Seriously? You make me taste a delicious wine but you can't sell it to me?" I finally negotiated with him to buy a case for my private collection. For the next three summers, I carefully rationed those twelve bottles, pouring Ivo's wine at rooftop picnics with other wine lovers whom I knew would appreciate it.

Blanc de noirs is a white wine made from a red grape, a technique you see all the time with Pinot Noir and Pinot Meunier in Champagne, where base wines are blended in the creation of a single wine. It is more unusual when a winemaker decides to make a blanc de noirs as a still wine. Here, red grapes are gently pressed just until very clear, pale juices run out of the fruit. Since the skin doesn't imprint any color or tannins, the wine expresses the aromatics of the grape, allowing the brightest, purest expression to come through. This is what makes it interesting to me: it's a different way to explore the taste of a grape.

Later, I was introduced to Espontaneo, a blanc de noirs made by Ludovic Engelvin, who also makes wine in the Languedoc. I remember having a similar kind of feeling as I did when drinking Ivo's wine. It was so delicious and incredible. Ludo is a fan of toreador culture, so he named the wine Espontaneo after the word for a village kid who jumps into a bull-fighting arena. In this way, this blanc de noirs made from a vineyard of Grenache Noir in the Languedoc was like the punk village kid who wants to catch the attention of others. That summer, I bought enough bottles to pour the 2014 vintage by the glass at La Buvette, and it became a favorite for the entire season. But the following year, Ludo lost a big part of the harvest and had to stop making blanc de noirs. It's only been recently that's he's started to make it again. Ivo doesn't make his blanc de noirs often, either. As he explains it, sometimes he wakes up too late, and the grapes have become too ripe for this style.

That's the tricky thing about loving this kind of wine. A still blanc de noirs from the south is rare, and the climate has to cooperate for it to be made: it is possible to make only when the harvest is good. Unfortunately, there aren't normal seasons anymore. Springs are early, but then it's possible to get hail in April when the vines are just starting to bud, killing the new growth. An early May frost can kill a whole harvest. There is no true lesson here except for the idea to appreciate and enjoy a rare wine, which may not be around forever.

ANYTIME RECIPES

Stocking my kitchen with a few simple, reliable ingredients makes it is easier to feed myself well at any time of the day or night. This chapter is dedicated to the kind of recipes that make use of what I usually already have on hand, whether in the refrigerator, on the shelf, or stashed in the freezer. They are also the kind of imprecise recipes that allow freedom to add more of a favorite ingredient or to be flexible with what you do have on hand. In other words, go ahead and add more butter, or mustard, or anchovies if you're so inclined.

EDAMAME HUMMUS

I've always loved hummus, especially because it reminds me of the time I spent living in the Middle East. Whether smeared on toasted bread or spooned onto a plate and topped with a salad of beets or sliced radishes, hummus can be more than a dip. It can also be made with ingredients beyond chickpeas and standard seasonings. Since I always have giant white beans at the shop, I've made "hummus" with those beans, mixing in a little rosemary with perfectly good results. And after coming home from a visit to the Asian markets in Belleville, I got it in my mind to try it with edamame. (Why not? Those are beans, too.) Here, I add a little tahini for tanginess and a little soy sauce for salt flavor, but the result isn't taken in either a Middle Eastern or Asian direction. Instead, it's a good example of making something familiar with a slight twist. Because edamame beans aren't as creamy as other kinds of beans, the texture is closer to a tapenade than a classic hummus.

Cook the edamame according to the directions on the package. Remove and discard the green exterior pods (I call these the "pajamas") until you have 2 cups of shelled beans. (You may have a bit extra.) Combine the beans in a food processor with the onion, garlic, lemon juice, tahini, soy sauce, and cumin. Pulse a few times, scraping down the sides of the food processor once or twice, until the edamame is a little smoother. With the processor running, drizzle in the oil and then continue to blend until well-blended. Serve with toasted bread. Leftovers keep in a sealed container in the refrigerator for 1 week.

MAKES ABOUT 1½ CUPS

1½ pounds frozen edamame*

¼ small yellow onion, coarsely chopped

1 garlic clove, coarsely chopped

¼ cup freshly squeezed lemon juice

1 tablespoon tahini

2 tablespoons soy sauce

1 teaspoon ground cumin

¼ cup extra-virgin olive oil

Toasted bread, for serving

You can save time by buying already-shelled edamame. A 12-ounce bag of frozen shelled edamame will be more than you need for this recipe.

MUSTARD VINAIGRETTE
TO MAKE A SALAD FOR ANY SEASON

My mum always made a simple mustard vinaigrette for us when I was growing up, and even today it is something that I make whenever I want a salad. In the winter, it is perfect with purple or pink chicory leaves and endive, while in the summer I add it to fresh tomatoes or green beans. For a classic bistro carrot salad (*carrottes râpées*), you can grate a carrot and mix it with this vinaigrette (When I make *carrottes râpées*, I like to add orange juice and zest, too). That's the great thing about this vinaigrette—it goes with any salad you happen to be in the mood to make.

This recipe is a starting point. To dress a salad with delicate lettuce leaves, like butter lettuce, I add a little more olive oil so the vinaigrette is looser and can lightly coat the leaves. For potato salad, I make the vinaigrette with a little less oil so that it is nearly as thick as mayonnaise. The creaminess of the vinaigrette comes from whisking the olive oil into the mustard, but sometimes I just put the ingredients in a jam jar and shake it up.

Combine the salt and pepper in a small bowl and pour in the vinegar so it dissolves the salt. Using a fork or small whisk, whisk in the mustard until smooth. Gradually drizzle in the olive oil while whisking until creamy. If you'd like, add a little more olive oil to make it creamier and milder. Taste and add a little bit of honey, if desired.

MAKES ½ CUP, ENOUGH FOR A WEEK'S WORTH OF SALADS

Pinch of sea salt

Pinch of freshly ground black pepper

2 tablespoons cider vinegar or red wine vinegar (nothing too fancy or strong)

¼ cup Dijon mustard*

¼ cup extra-virgin olive oil, or more if desired

Honey (optional)

I tend to prefer a smooth mustard that is not too strong, such as a classic smooth moutarde de Dijon, but a more coarsely ground mustard offers a more textured vinaigrette with a sharper finish.

SARDINES, BUTTER, AND BURNT LEMON

I always stock my pantry with cans of sardines, a habit I've had ever since I was a student. It was cheap and effortless, and even though today I know enough to choose better-quality sardines, the cans I buy are still quite affordable.

A few years ago, I was invited by Andrew Tarlow and Lee Desrosiers to do an event at Achilles Heel in Brooklyn. Behind the bar was a courtyard with a fire pit and grill, which became the heart of the event. I was so inspired by this new environment that I spent some time thinking about how I could twist the little Parisian thing I do at La Buvette to show a sense of place. The answers lay in the fire: I wrapped pears in foil and cooked them in ashes for a cheese plate and Lee even smoked my Chou Farci (page 172) in the fire, too. As for my plate of sardines, I took a lemon half and put it in the fire to burn. The results—juice that was slightly sweeter and less acidic, with a touch of charred lemon flavor—changed the fish just enough to taste like something new. Now when I'm at home, I often take a few more minutes to burn a lemon half in a pan. To relive that memory of one of my most enjoyable dinners ever, the few extra minutes of preparation is worth it.

Heat a skillet over medium-high heat. Put the lemon halves, cut-side down, in the pan and sear until the lemon halves turn deeply caramelized on the cut sides, about 3 minutes. Let cool.

If the sardines are quite large, you may want to pry them open and lift out the backbones, though it is not necessary to do so for smaller fish (the bones are soft enough to eat). Regardless, preserve the shape of the fish.

Set a plate with butter, bread, sardines, and lemon and assemble as desired, adding a pinch of salt if you'd like.

SERVES 1 OR MORE

1 lemon, halved

1 can sardines*

A generous pat of salted butter or Seaweed Butter (page 71)

A couple of slices of sourdough or levain-style bread

Flaky sea salt, such as Maldon (optional), for seasoning

I avoid the tomato- and chile-flavored versions of canned sardines, always sticking with the classic, extra-virgin olive-oil or extra-virgin olive oil and lemon options so I can taste the sardine flavor.

VINS OUILLÉS

The year after I started La Buvette, some of my friends opened up Le Mary Celeste, one of the first cocktail bars in Paris to have a great wine list *and* delicious food. At the time, a cocktail bar in Paris that pleased wine people and food people was rare—either the food wasn't good or you couldn't get any decent wine to drink. But this place did everything well—and was open late enough that I could go after work. For a whole summer, I went there to eat oysters and drink wine—specifically a bottle called Fleur de Savagnin, made by Julien and Charline Labet. I became so obsessed with this wine that I begged the sommelier to take it off the wine list so it wouldn't sell out before my next visit.

This wine comes from the Jura, a region tucked just below mountains in an eastern corner of France. Even though wine has been made here for centuries, wine production remains quite small and had fallen out of favor until fairly recently as more people started rediscovering its wines. Now the wines from this area have become quite fashionable. Pinot Noir and Chardonnay grow here, as well as the light red grape Trousseau. But the interesting grape to me is Savagnin, an ancient variety (and progenitor of much better-known grapes, including Sauvignon). Despite this grape's centuries-old lineage, Savagnin rarely grows anywhere else. It has a natural bright acidity and is traditionally used to make *vin jaune* (yellow wine), an oxidative style that takes six years of aging in barrels before it's ready to be bottled. During that time, some of the wine evaporates from the barrels, exposing the remaining wine to air and allowing a thin veil of yeast to form on the top. The result is a wine that is a little like sherry—rich with flavors of hazelnuts, toasted bread, honey, and spices; it's the kind of bottle I would open only with the intention of

118

LA BUVETTE

sharing it with five or six friends. It's so complex that one glass on a special occasion sipped alongside something strong, like a crazy blue cheese, is the most classic way to enjoy this wine. So no, *vin jaune* was not the wine that I was drinking that summer.

Instead of letting the wine evaporate for the veil of yeast to form, Julien makes Fleur de Savagnin in a style called *vins ouillés*, wines that are "filled up." He tops off the barrels with wine that he has reserved to avoid the formation of the oxidative veil. Without the veil and the six years of mandatory aging, the result is entirely different—a younger, fresher expression of Savagnin, which is something that I could still drink all summer or any time of the year.

GREEN BEAN, PEACH, AND ALMOND SALAD

Cooking in the summer can be so simple, a time when much of what I want to eat requires little to no preparation. This salad comes from a summer vacation in Ibiza. We stayed near an almond orchard, and I became obsessed with fresh almonds, spending hours removing the fuzzy green skins so everyone could enjoy the white nuts. When it was my turn to make a salad for dinner, I grabbed a handful of these nuts to pair with the fresh local produce, which happened to be white peaches and green beans. Even though it came from the very innocent idea of using what I had, it has become one of my classic summer salads, something that everyone loves.

With a salad as simple as this, I prefer to display the ingredients nicely and to spoon the vinaigrette over the top à la minute or serve the vinaigrette on the side so people can season their salad as they like.

Bring a pot of salted water to a boil over high heat. Add the green beans and cook until tender but still crisp, 3 to 4 minutes. Drain the beans in a colander and run cold water over them to cool them down. If it's a very hot day, consider giving them a soak in ice water to ensure they stay crisp.

Put the green beans in a bowl or platter and add the peaches and almonds on top. Serve on the table with the vinaigrette and sea salt so people can season as they like.

SERVES 4

2 pounds green beans, trimmed

Salt

4 white peaches or donut peaches, cut into wedges

½ cup peeled fresh almonds (just the inside white nut, not the green fuzzy part)*

½ cup Mustard Vinaigrette (page 115)

Flaky sea salt, such as Maldon, for seasoning

If you can't find green almonds or if peach season doesn't overlap with green almond season, substitute toasted Marcona almonds. It won't be quite as special as a salad made with fresh almonds, but it is still a nice combination.

TOMATO, OREGANO, AND BERRY SALAD

Currants remind me of my childhood in the Loire Valley, where I would eat them straight out of our yard. Even though the season for currants is short, I always try to use them in as many ways as possible when they're available, including in this tomato salad. But while I adore currants, other tart berries work as well. Blackberries are juicy and give the salad a dramatic look (if they are quite large, cut them in half), while gooseberries add a little pop of bright flavor. The key is picking a berry that isn't too sweet so it complements the tomatoes. If your tomatoes are exceptionally juicy, sop up the extra juices left in the salad bowl with bread. If you happen to live in a coastal area and come across sea beans, they also make a nice saline, crunchy accent to this simple recipe.

Combine the tomatoes, berries, and oregano in a bowl and season with a generous pinch of salt. Serve on the table with the vinaigrette and salt so people can season as they like.

SERVES 4

4 to 5 large tomatoes, cut into chunks (about 4 cups)

½ cup tart berries, such as fresh red currants, blackberries, raspberries, or gooseberries

1 tablespoon fresh oregano leaves (from about 2 sprigs)

Flaky sea salt, such as Maldon, for seasoning

½ cup Mustard Vinaigrette (page 115)

When I first opened La Buvette, I sold bottles of Le Verre des Poètes, a wine made by Emile Heredia with a rare grape called Pineau d'Aunis. It was a beautiful light red wine that gave an impression of white pepper, and though Emile has since sold the vineyard, I still think of this wine when I think of Pineau d'Aunis.

With French grapes, most people know the classic varieties that are famous all over the world—Chardonnay, Sauvignon, Cabernet, Pinot Noir, and so forth. But as natural winemakers have taken a closer look into the history of the land they farm, they are also revitalizing forgotten grape varieties that were nearly lost, either because they were pulled out in favor of more popular grapes or because they weren't vigorous enough to produce at a high yield.

This is the case with Pineau d'Aunis, a traditional grape of the Loire Valley that was called Chenin Noir for most of the twentieth century to avoid confusion with Pinot grapes in Bourgogne (Burgundy). A few decades ago, it was on the verge of disappearing because, like other forgotten French grapes such as Grolleau and Romorantin, Pineau d'Aunis vines were not productive enough to make profits for the farmers. But now a new generation of winemakers is placing more value on biodiversity, stopping the decline of these varieties. Through those efforts, they've also restored the original Pineau d'Aunis name.

Rather than being a concentrated wine, Pineau d'Aunis makes an elegant and light wine that is never all that structured. If I see a cuvée on a wine list that is made with this grape from a winemaker I like, I always order it.

THE SECRET WORLD OF RUNGIS

I met Jane Drotter years ago when she owned Yard, a restaurant not too far from La Buvette. One Monday evening, we were chatting at the bar when she told me that she was leaving at 3 a.m. to pick up ingredients and supplies at Rungis, one of the most impressive international wholesale markets in the world. But on that night, she was having a hard time finding available staff to make the trip with her.

Rungis is more than a market. Located 7 kilometers outside of Paris on the way to Orly Airport, it is a city within a city—large enough to have its own post office and police. Without Rungis, there is no food in Paris. It's there that wheels of fresh cheese from the French countryside and fish caught at sea are sold to distributors who will truck them to all corners of Europe. Anything and everything you could possibly need for a restaurant kitchen you will find in one of the sprawling halls.

No matter how impressive and comprehensive Rungis can be, waking up at 3 a.m. to buy supplies takes rare commitment from restaurant people who work late into the evening. Those who skip the journey can order ingredients from a food delivery company, but then they don't get to choose the ingredients themselves. Adeline Grattard, the chef of Yam'Tcha who cooks from a French-Chinese perspective, goes to Rungis because she doesn't want anyone else choosing ingredients for her. The same is true for some bistro owners, such as Raquel Carena of Le Baratin and Jane while she owned Yard.

Jane would go with a different cook every week to help collect and load all of the produce and meat, but that week no one was free. Since La Buvette was closed the next day, I told Jane that it would give me great pleasure to join her.

That marked the first of what became a Monday ritual of visiting Rungis: I enjoyed it so much that I told her I could come any time.

In the early morning hours, there is such a special mood at Rungis. It's almost as if it's an alternative world that operates only at night, with huge trucks dwarfing cars and competing for space at loading docks. It can be an intimidating place if you don't know where you are going.

Jane learned how to navigate Rungis with the help of other restaurant owners and chefs who made introductions to their meat and produce vendors. There is solidarity among those who go to Rungis, as if they are part of a particular kind of night life—not for partying but for working while everyone else is sleeping. Our routine was always the same: After paying a toll at the entrance, we pulled Jane's tiny truck next to one of the pavilions specializing in meat and picked up the white coats required for entering. Then we walked past endless stalls of offal before arriving at the poultry pavilion. Once the meat was loaded into Jane's truck, we took a little break Le Saint Hubert for a coffee and croissant. There, men in white coats who had been up all night butchering meat ordered beer or wine to drink with their meal.

Then we drove to the organic produce pavilion to pick up the vegetables and everything else Jane needed. We ended the morning at the flower pavilion, where we treated ourselves to an armful of flowers. Jane said it was her reward for working in such early hours; she loved waking up after a Rungis morning to an apartment filled with flowers. At the time, I lived near the Marche d'Aligre, so after Jane and I unloaded the ingredients—anything from 50 kilos of potatoes to heavy containers of oil—we would stop at a bakery called Blé Sucré for an apple pastry and a little more coffee, and then we'd go home to sleep.

When Jane sold Yard in 2017, we quickly realized how much we missed our Rungis ritual. Through those experiences, the moments we shared in those early mornings, we became closer friends. Now, every so often, we look for an occasion to pay the crazy wholesale market another visit to come home with armfuls of flowers and plenty of cherries to pickle.

A REALLY BUTTERY CROQUE MONSIEUR

This sandwich represents a simple taste of childhood, something my mum made for lunch for me and my brother when we were growing up. I have to confess that the combination of ham and melting cheese on buttery, soft white bread tastes just as good as an adult, particularly after drinking too much wine. When friends who used to live around the corner from La Buvette got married, my friend Alix Lacloche and I made these sandwiches for everyone as a late-night bite to eat.

The best way to make a croque monsieur is to buy sliced white bread (we call it "American bread" in France) and butter it really well before griddling the sandwiches. I prefer to make the sandwich on small slices of bread so I can eat two sandwiches instead of one. The best croque will have fancy cheese and ham, but this is not always about being fancy.

Brush both sides of each piece of bread generously with butter. (This is a really buttery croque monsieur after all!) Lay out all of the pieces of bread. On 4 of the pieces, place 1 piece of cheese, followed by 1 piece of ham, followed by 1 piece of cheese (that way the ham is in the center). Top with the remaining bread.

Heat a griddle or skillet over medium heat. In batches, cook the sandwiches until the bread is evenly browned and the cheese is completely melted. If the bread is getting dark but the cheese hasn't started melting, turn the heat to low and continue to griddle, gently turning the sandwiches over for even cooking. Serve hot.

SERVES 4 (2 IF YOU ARE EXTRA HUNGRY)

½ cup salted butter, melted

8 slices classic white sandwich bread or pain de mie

8 slices Comté or tomme or another good melting cheese (about 6 ounces)*

4 slices ham

*For the best results, buy a cheese that melts easily, which means Comté or tomme in France, but could mean Monterey Jack in America. Avoid cheeses like aged Cheddar, which is a little too sharp for the sandwich.

LA BUVETTE

ANCHOVY, EGG YOLK, AND HAZELNUT PASTA

My absolute favorite pasta is carbonara, and one night I came home with an intense craving for it. Even though I was absolutely dying to make carbonara, I didn't have the right ingredients. So I thought I might be able to get that satisfaction of salty, creamy noodles in a different way. I looked around for what I did have: a bit of cream, some eggs, some dried pasta, a can of anchovies, and my beloved hazelnuts. And even though it wasn't carbonara, it was what I needed that night. I now make this without measuring, and if I am very hungry, I simply add more pasta to the pot.

In a small saucepan, combine the anchovies, cream, and pepper and warm over medium heat. The anchovies often start to melt in the sauce as they warm up, but you can help the process along by pressing the anchovies with a fork as they heat. Once the cream begins to bubble on the edges, turn off the heat and pulse a couple of times with an immersion blender or use a wooden spoon to break up the anchovies and make the sauce smoother. Cover to keep the sauce warm.

While the cream and anchovies cook together, bring a pot of salted water to a boil. Cook the pasta according to the instructions on the package. While the pasta cooks, have the yolks ready to go. (I prop the yolks up in their shells so they are easy to slide on top of the finished pasta.)

Drain the noodles in a colander and then return them to the pot. Pour the sauce over the noodles and stir well to combine. Divide the pasta between two bowls and sprinkle with hazelnuts. Place a yolk on top of each bowl and serve immediately.

SERVES 2

1 (2-ounce) can anchovies, drained

½ cup heavy cream (if you are a real cream lover, add a little more)

¼ teaspoon freshly ground black pepper

8 ounces fettuccine or another dry noodle pasta

2 egg yolks

¼ cup chopped lightly toasted hazelnuts

LE GOÛTER

Le goûter is the French expression for afternoon tea or snack, the unofficial fourth meal of the day, and it is nearly always something sweet. As a child, I ate chocolate with bread, a treat I still love to indulge in when I have just enough chocolate mousse left from dessert the day before to smear onto a crunchy baguette. Or sometimes my mum would let us have bread with jam. When I was a kid, *le goûter* was a treat after school, in between playtime or homework and dinner. I still think of it as little treat in the afternoon, and I like to keep it sweet because I have a *bec à sucré* (sugar beak, which means the kind of person who always likes to eat something sweet.)

BAGUETTE + JAM

Eating a baguette with butter and jam for breakfast or *le goûter* is absolutely a classic French thing to do, but for whatever reason, I just cannot eat jam with butter. I love the very simple taste of jam with bread *or* butter with bread, just not all three. This doesn't mean that butter and jam are wrong in any way; it's just not for me. But I truly have always loved jam. My mum always made her own batches, and she would let me participate. I can still remember standing on a little special stool in the kitchen so I could reach the stove, helping her stir the pot to feel as if I was helping. Today I make my own jam, experimenting with flavors that are still sweet enough for *le goûter* but have a different character from classic versions with additions of spices or herbs.

Making Homemade Jam

The best jam comes from in-season fruit. What makes the jam taste great is the ripeness of the fruit, and most of the time I'd rather make jam with fruit that is slightly too ripe than too green. Even if the fruit doesn't look nice, if it is ripe and in season, it will make delicious jam. I add pectin so I don't have to add as much sugar as traditional jams (pectin helps thicken jam in place of sugar).

There is a difference between the method I use for preparing jam for storage and the approved method for canning in America. While both begin with sanitized glass jars (which are washed and then kept warm in a pot of hot water), the difference comes once the jars are filled. When the jam is hot, I cap each jar and turn it upside down so that as the jar cools, it forms a vacuum that seals the lid. I've never had a problem with spoilage using this method, but American regulations advise that the jam-filled jars must be boiled in hot water for 5 to 10 minutes before they can be stored at room temperature. Otherwise, they recommend storing the jam in the refrigerator. For this reason, store the jam in the refrigerator or look up guidelines on how to process jams in a boiling water bath. I recycle glass jars from other jam-making projects, but it's a good idea to use a new lid each time. When making jam in America, use 1-cup or 1-pint canning jars; hardware stores are a good place to find a range of canning supplies.

MUM'S SPECIAL PEAR
AND FRESH GINGER JAM

When I was a teen, my mum began turning her creativity to the kitchen, experimenting with new flavors and trying out recipes she had never made before. This jam, a combination of grated pear and fresh ginger, was such a success that it has become her signature preserve. A range of pears work well in this jam, but bigger, rounder Comice pears are a good place to start. Use fruit that is ripe but not so soft that it is impossible to grate. While I've tried out different versions of this recipe, such as swapping ginger out for timut pepper, the original remains my favorite.

In a small bowl, whisk together the sugar and pectin.

With the largest holes of a box grater, grate the pears (with their skins) directly into a pot or saucepan (use what you will cook the jam in). Stop once you grate close enough to the stem and core and discard them. (You'll have about 4 cups of grated pear.) Mix in the ginger and lemon.

Sprinkle the pectin sugar in an even layer over the fruit and let sit for at least 30 minutes or up to a couple of hours at room temperature. The pears may turn a bit brown, but that's okay.

Put a plate in the refrigerator to chill. Put four 8-ounce jars in a pot large enough to hold them and cover with water. Bring the pot to a simmer over high heat, then turn the heat off and leave the jars in the water to keep them hot.

Stir the pectin sugar into the pears and bring to a boil. Lower the heat to medium and cook until the juices begin to thicken, about 10 minutes. You'll notice that the bubbles will start to become thicker and larger as the jam thickens. At this point, dab a spoonful onto the chilled plate to see if it stays in its place and doesn't run off when the plate is held at an angle. Turn off the heat. To make the jam just a bit smoother, pulse it one or two times with an immersion blender to break apart some of the pear while leaving some of the texture in place (this step is optional).

Spread a towel on the counter. Using tongs, pull the jars out of the water and place on the towel. Fill the jars with the jam and cool to room temperature, then cap the jars and refrigerate for up to 4 months. The ginger flavor will taste stronger the day after.

MAKES ABOUT 4 CUPS

1½ cups sugar

2 tablespoons powdered pectin

2¼ pounds pears (about 6 large pears)

1 tablespoon grated fresh ginger

Juice of 1 lemon (about 3 tablespoons)

FIG AND SAGE JAM

Fig season is very short, and the shorter the window for buying delicious figs, the more I want to preserve as much of the fruit as possible. I especially love to use figs that are on the edge of being too ripe, almost to the point that they taste like jam even before they're cooked. To counter a little bit of that sweetness, I add fresh sage leaves, finding that the sharpness of the herb balances out the sweetness of the fruit. You can use either green or black figs: I have a slight preference for black figs, but I find that green figs have softer skins and make a smoother jam.

In a small bowl, whisk together the sugar and pectin.

Halve the figs, removing any tough stems. Put the figs in a medium pot or saucepan (use what you will cook the jam in). Stir in the lemon juice and sage. Sprinkle the pectin sugar in an even layer over the fruit and let sit for at least 30 minutes or up to a couple of hours at room temperature.

Put a plate in the refrigerator to chill. Put four 8-ounce jars in a pot large enough to hold them and cover with water. Bring the pot to a simmer over high heat, then turn the heat off and leave the jars in the water to keep them hot.

Stir the pectin sugar into the figs and bring to a boil. Lower the heat to medium and cook until the juices begin to thicken, 12 to 20 minutes depending on the ripeness of the figs. You'll notice that the bubbles will start to become thicker and larger as the jam thickens. At this point, dab a spoonful onto the chilled plate to see if it stays in place and runs only slightly when the plate is held at an angle. Remove the sage leaves. To make the jam just a bit smoother, pulse it one or two times with an immersion blender to break apart some of the fig pieces, while leaving some of the texture in place (this step is optional).

Spread a towel on the counter. Using tongs, pull the jars out of the water and place on the towel. Fill the jars with the jam and cool to room temperature, then cap the jars and refrigerate for up to 4 months.

MAKES ABOUT 4 CUPS

1½ cups sugar

2 tablespoons powdered pectin

2 pounds fresh black or green figs (it doesn't matter what color as long as they are ripe)

Juice of 2 lemons (about ⅓ cup)

3 sprigs fresh sage

CIDER

While I used to be very shy about drinking wine, I never was shy about cider. When I was a kid, my parents allowed me to have a sip whenever we were eating buckwheat crepes, which is a traditional pairing in Normandy and Brittany. Those ciders weren't anything special, but they were sparkling, a little sweet, quite low in alcohol, and very easy to drink.

Even though I've always liked cider, I didn't pay much attention to it professionally until we started serving cider at Le Dauphin. Cyril Zangs had started to introduce his craft ciders to restaurants in Paris. He was one of the first to take it seriously, making very dry, natural ciders that were as concentrated and complex as the wines we served at the bar. His bottles made a case in Paris that serious wine drinkers should also drink cider.

It was after I tried Cyril's ciders that I was introduced to Trois Pépins (meaning "the three seeds"), a cider from Jacques Perritaz of Cidrerie du Vulcain from Fribourg, Switzerland. The three seeds of the name refers to the apple, pear, and quince blended together to make the cider. On my first taste, it blew my mind, hitting all corners of my mouth. The apple gave it dryness and structure while the pear created a round sweetness. The third seed, the quince, was the aromatic expression, giving the cider a long finish.

Today, cider can come in many styles, from dry to the edge of sweetness, making it the perfect choice for those times when you want a little something to drink, but it feels too early to have something like wine—like late Sunday afternoons, or with your *goûter*—or after waking up after a late night when you feel like you probably shouldn't be drinking anything at all. In these cases, and so many others, cider is nearly always the right choice to me.

WHITE PEACH AND VERBENA JAM

Fresh lemon verbena has a citrusy, floral aroma that is amazing with delicate white peaches. Verbena leaves are not the easiest to find in shops, but the herb grows easily in gardens in the countryside (but not on Paris balconies because they need more outdoor space and fresh air). When you do find some lemon verbena, let the leaves dry. You can use fresh or dry leaves for this jam. If you have extra verbena leaves, steep them in hot water for an herbal tea. The best peaches for this jam are those flat white peaches, which I was surprised to learn are called "donut peaches" in America! If you cannot find them, round white peaches work fine. This jam is stored in the refrigerator and eaten within a couple of months, since white peaches are low in pectin and acidity and tend to not keep as well as other fruit jams.

In a small bowl, whisk together the sugar and pectin.

If the peaches are very ripe, you can peel the skin off by hand. If the skin is stubborn, try this trick: cut the peaches in half and place in a single layer, skin-side up, in a heatproof casserole. Pour boiling water over the peaches and let them sit until cool enough to touch. Pick up a peach and peel off the skin by hand. Remove the pits and cut the peaches into quarters. You will have about 4 cups.

Put the peaches in a pot or saucepan (use what you will cook the jam in). With a strainer to avoid getting seeds in the jam, squeeze the lemons over the peaches and add the lemon halves to the saucepan. Add the verbena leaves and stir everything together. Sprinkle the pectin sugar in an even layer over the fruit and let sit for at least 30 minutes or up to a couple of hours at room temperature.

Put a plate in the refrigerator to chill. Put three 8-ounce jars in a pot large enough to hold them and cover with water. Bring the pot to a simmer over high heat, then turn the heat off and leave the jars in the water to keep them hot.

MAKES ABOUT 3 CUPS

1¼ cups sugar

2 tablespoons powdered pectin

2 pounds white peaches (opt for flat donut peaches, if available; they are very sweet)*

2 lemons, halved

5 to 6 lemon verbena leaves, fresh or dried

White peaches are generally not acidic enough on their own for water-bath canning according to American guidelines. Store this jam in the refrigerator.

Stir the pectin sugar into the peaches and bring the peaches to a boil. Lower the heat to medium and cook gently until the juices begin to thicken, about 10 minutes. You'll notice that the bubbles will start to become thicker and larger as the jam thickens. At this point, dab a spoonful onto the chilled plate to see if it stays in place and doesn't run off when the plate is held at an angle. Remove the lemon halves and verbena leaves. To make the jam just a bit smoother, pulse it one or two times with an immersion blender to break apart some of the peaches while keeping some of the texture in place (this step is optional).

Spread a towel on the counter. Using tongs, pull the jars out of the water and place on the towel. Fill the jars with the jam and cool to room temperature, then cap them and refrigerate for up to 2 months. The top may brown a little, but that's okay—the jam is still perfectly safe to eat.

A VERY CLASSIC FRUIT CAKE

When I was a kid, our family spent almost every Sunday at my grandparents' house in the countryside, but it wasn't something my brother and I looked forward to. My grandparents, who were farmers, experienced a family tragedy years ago and they never seemed to regain their happiness. For me and my brother, Sundays were always same: we'd tour around the garden and play with my father's old toys before we all sat down to meal that seemed to drag on forever. At this point in the story, you may expect me to say that at least the meals were incredible, but my grandmother preferred to buy prepared meals from a *traiteur* (a shop specializing in ready-to-eat food) than to cook herself. Even the dessert she served came from a shop. But the highlight of our Sunday routine was this fruit cake (pictured, page 144), the only thing she seemed to make for us. She always gave it to us as we said good-bye, and when we got home in time for *goûter*, we would fight over who got the slice with the biggest pieces of red cherry.

I never knew why this was the only thing she made for us, or why we never ate it with her. Maybe for my grandmother, who had a hard life and was a sad person, making this cake for us to bring home was her way of showing how much she loved us. This is the only recipe I have from her, and for this reason it's quite special to me. The classic fruit mix from my grandmother was cherries, angelica, orange peel, and raisins. Over the years, I've improvised with hazelnuts, candied ginger, dried cranberries, and apricots, so use a combination that delights you.

Put the dried fruit in a small saucepan and pour the whiskey over the top. Bring to a simmer briefly, then turn off the heat and let the fruit soak to plump up, about 20 minutes. Cut the candied fruits into ¼- to ½-inch pieces.

MAKES ONE 9 BY 5-INCH LOAF CAKE, ABOUT 8 SERVINGS

½ cup chopped mixed dried fruits (any combination of raisins, golden raisins, dried cranberries, and/or dried diced apricots)

¼ cup whiskey

½ cup candied fruits (candied cherries, candied orange peel, candied ginger, candied angelica, or a combination)

½ cup salted butter, at room temperature

¾ cup sugar

3 eggs

1½ cups all-purpose flour

½ teaspoon baking powder

½ teaspoon baking soda

¼ teaspoon fine sea salt

½ cup chopped lightly toasted hazelnuts

Butter a 9 by 5-inch loaf pan and then dust with flour, shaking out the excess. Preheat the oven to 350°F.

In a large bowl, mix the butter with a rubber spatula to ensure it's soft and malleable. Add the sugar and mix until the sugar is evenly incorporated. One by one, mix in the eggs, mixing well between additions, until evenly incorporated.

In a separate bowl, whisk together the flour, baking powder, baking soda, and salt.

Drain the dried fruit, saving any soaking liquid that remains behind. Dust the soaked fruit and candied fruit in a little of the flour mixture (this prevents the fruit pieces from falling to the bottom of the cake while baking).

In the bowl with the butter and eggs, add the flour mixture in three parts, gently stirring between additions to completely incorporate. Fold in the dried fruit, candied fruit, and nuts until evenly incorporated, then stir in the soaking liquid.

Spoon the batter into the prepared pan and bake until a knife inserted into the center of the loaf comes out clean and the top has browned nicely, about 55 minutes. (I like this fruit cake best when the crust is dark brown and well-cooked.) Let cool, then wrap it up in parchment paper or plastic wrap. The fruit cake is better the day after it's baked, but it lasts on the counter for up to a week.

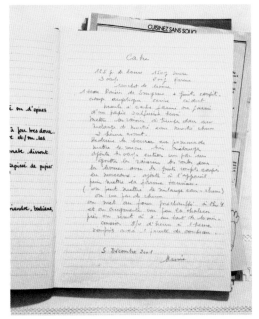

ROSE, CUMIN, AND APRICOT SABLÉS

The idea for these sablés came about one sunny day when my friends and I were taking part in a *vide-grenier* (empty the attic), a neighborhood sidewalk sale. Friends had asked if I'd help sell their couch, which was perfect because we would have a place to sit before we sold it. On this afternoon, Frédérick Grasser-Hermé came to say hello with a new tart from Pierre Hermé, her ex-husband, who is still a good friend of hers. That afternoon, he had been experimenting with new flavors and gave the tart to Frédérick to see what she thought. When she saw us, she offered to share it, so there we were, sitting on an old couch in the middle of the sidewalk, eating this incredible tart. It was well baked but not burned and featured unpeeled peach halves sitting on top of a rose-infused almond cream. Cumin-caramelized sugar drizzled on top was the finishing touch. Even though Frédérick said the tart was just an experiment, I thought it had such incomparable flavors matches as to be unforgettable.

It's easy to think that it was the occasion—the sunny day, the time spent with friends, the delight of eating a special tart on an old couch on the sidewalk—that made the flavors so memorable, but I never forgot those flavor combinations and wanted to make my own tribute to that experience. Since the tart was too complicated for me, I created a recipe based on Pierre Hermé's recipe for sablés to capture the flavors of the original tart. I could have used candied peaches to be literal about everything, but dried apricots are a million times easier to find and make a result that is just as charming.

CONTINUED

In a large bowl, mix the butter with a rubber spatula to ensure it's soft and malleable. Add ⅓ cup of the sugar and mix until the sugar is evenly incorporated.

In a smaller bowl, whisk together the flour, cumin, and sea salt. Add the flour to the butter mixture in three parts, gently stirring in between additions to completely mix in. Stir in the apricots until incorporated. On a lightly dusted counter, roll and pat the dough into a sausage shape about 1½ inches in diameter. Wrap in plastic wrap, twisting the ends tightly. Refrigerate for at least 2 hours, or until firm. (You can do this a couple of days ahead.)

Preheat the oven to 350°F. Line a couple of baking sheets with parchment paper.

Crush the rosebuds with your hands and mix them into the remaining 2 tablespoons sugar. (You can do this a couple of days ahead for a deeper rose flavor. If the rosebuds are not dry enough to crush by hand, try pulsing them with the sugar in a spice grinder.)

With a sharp knife, cut the dough into ½-inch-thick coins or slightly thinner. Roll the edges of each coin in the rose sugar and set about 1 inch apart on the prepared pans.

Bake each pan, rotating once, until the bottom and edges have lightly browned but before the apricots on the surface become too dark, 18 to 20 minutes. Let the sablés cool completely on the baking sheets. Once cool, store them in a tin for 1 week, but you will have finished them before then.

MAKES ABOUT
24 COOKIES

¾ cup salted butter,
at room temperature

⅓ cup plus 2 tablespoons
sugar

1½ cups all-purpose flour

½ teaspoon ground cumin

¼ teaspoon flaky sea salt,
such as Maldon

½ cup finely diced dried
apricots

10 dehydrated rosebuds,
green stem ends removed

NEW-STYLE
NÉGOCIANT

In 2011, Jean-Pascal Sarnin and Jean-Marie Berrux vinified Pinot Noir grapes from a parcel of land in Bourgogne. Even though only 600 magnums of the wine were made, this cuvée quickly became one of La Buvette's most iconic (and largest) bottles, illustrating the ways in which people who don't own vineyards can make memorable wine in France today.

In a way, this is actually an old idea. It used to be that *négociants*, the people who buy grapes to make wine rather than growing their own—used to control the wine industry in Bourgogne. In the twentieth century, this changed as more growers started bottling their own wine, ending their reliance on *négociants*. After a while, wine lovers came to believe that wine from a *négociant* was never going to be as good as wine from the people who worked the land.

Today, however, land in Bourgogne is so expensive that it's nearly impossible for new winemakers to buy even the tiniest vineyard. So if you are a couple of winemaking guys in Bourgogne without a vineyard, and you hear about a winemaker who farms in a healthy way and has more grapes than he can use, you're going to call him up and ask if you can buy the extra fruit. That was the case with this wine: Jean-Pascal Sarnin and Jean-Marie Berrux didn't own land in Bourgogne; they bought grapes that otherwise would have been sold to a wine cooperative or elsewhere.

These new-style *négociants* know how their grapes were farmed, and sometimes they even work the land themselves. They simply do not own it, and in this way, they are more free to play with different grapes and terroirs. This also means that a wine may be made in small quantities, and only once or twice, which brings me back to that bottle of Sarnin Berrux. The winemakers recognized that the Pinot Noir from the 2011 harvest was evolving into a special wine, so they bottled it in magnums to allow the wine to age in a longer, more elegant way. They even asked their neighbor, artist Matt McClune, to paint each label by hand.

I was permitted to buy only twelve bottles for the shop, but even so, it quickly became the Sunday night special, the bottle opened among wine industry friends who came to La Buvette on their night off. Each time a bottle was emptied, I saved the label, writing down the date and people who shared it with me and then decorating the shelves with the paintings. It became such an iconic bottle for Sunday night that the winemakers finally let me buy a few cases, but the bottles didn't last long. Every year I'd ask the winemakers when they might make it again, but they never did until 2015. We hosted the release party in December 2017, and that's the last time I've been able to get that wine into the shop.

That's the tricky thing with the new *négociant* model: no wine is guaranteed to be made year after year. Maybe a harvest fails to meet expectations or the winemakers move on to other projects. Regardless, I'm fortunate to have the memories of sharing Sarnin Berrux on those special Sundays.

MORE TIME
FOR COOKING

Any small moment—a dinner at home or a picnic on a river—
can be turned into an occasion with some attention and care in the
details. Even a meal of leftovers can be made better if I take the
time to spread out a tablecloth and pick out a couple of nice plates.
It is really about my own pleasure, too. Even if it's not exactly a
conscious decision, I always like to add a little something to ordinary evenings that I know will make someone happy. This chapter
is just about to make a meal just a little more special. You may be
cooking for your friends, your lover, your parents, or a very important guest whom you don't know all that well but hope to soon.
With these recipes you're going to spend a little more time in the
kitchen, but none of them are too professional or technical—
they're about celebrating the simple pleasures of cooking at home.

PIZZETTES IN THREE STYLES

When I met Alix Lacloche, an amazing chef in Paris, we discovered that we had a common passion for picnics. We spent a whole summer having picnics in parks or on my rooftop. One day, she made these lemon pizzettes, which I loved so much that I started requesting them for every outdoor occasion we planned together. This recipe is adapted from Alix's very nice cookbook, *Dans Ma Cuisine.* What makes these pizzettes good for picnics is their size—they are smaller than the size of your hand and hold their shape without becoming too soft in the center.

While I still love the lemon version, I also like to top some of the pizzettes with ricotta and herbs and others with anchovies. The dough makes enough for twelve portions, which is plenty for exploring the different topping options. To proceed, make the dough the day before you plan to bake the pizzettes. To make it even easier, you can buy dough from your favorite pizza place (which is what I do nine times out of ten when I make this recipe). While the dough is coming to room temperature, prepare the toppings, which make enough for four pizzettes of each version. If you want to make only one type of topping, adjust the quantities accordingly—it's a very forgiving recipe.

To make the dough, put the yeast in a small bowl and pour the water over it. Stir in the honey. Combine the flour and salt in a large bowl. Pour in the yeast mixture and begin to mix with your fingers until a shaggy dough forms. Put a kitchen towel over the bowl and let it rest for 20 minutes (this will allow the flour to absorb more of the water).

Sprinkle the counter with flour. Take the dough out of the bowl and knead it, pulling it, folding it, pressing it, and then repeating, for 7 to 10 minutes, until the dough becomes smooth and a little soft.

CONTINUED

MAKES 12 PIZZETTES

Dough

1 teaspoon instant yeast

1⅓ cups water, at room temperature

1 teaspoon honey

3¼ cups all-purpose flour

1½ teaspoons fine sea salt

Lemon Topping

Extra-virgin olive oil, for brushing and drizzling

1 organic lemon, very thinly sliced crosswise, seeds removed

1 tablespoon dried oregano, or 1 tablespoon crushed fennel seeds

Flaky sea salt, such as Maldon, for seasoning

Oil a large bowl that will fit in the refrigerator and put the dough inside. Cover and refrigerate for at least 12 hours or up to 24 hours. Before proceeding to shape and bake pizzettes, take the dough out of the refrigerator and let it come to room temperature for 2 hours.

Dust the counter with flour and cut the dough into twelve equal pieces. Using the palm of your hand, roll the dough into small balls and then cover with a clean kitchen towel and let rest for 30 minutes. The dough will puff up a bit while you prep the toppings.

If you have a pizza stone, place it on the bottom oven rack. (The pizza stone will give the bottom of the pizzettes a crispier crust, but you don't need one to make this recipe.) Preheat the oven to 500°F.** Have two 13 by 18-inch rimmed baking sheets ready.

For each pizzette, press the dough out with your palm or use a rolling pin on the floured countertop until the piece is a circle 4 to 5 inches wide. Put the dough onto a baking sheet and brush with olive oil. Repeat with the remaining dough, placing six rounds of dough (or as many as you can fit without touching) on each baking sheet. (If they don't all fit, you can always reload one of the baking sheets and bake in three batches.)

For the lemon pizzettes, put 1 large or 2 small lemon slices in the center of each dough round, leaving just enough to cover the surface but leave a crust. Brush the top with more olive oil and then finish with generous pinches of oregano and salt.

For the ricotta pizzettes, put ¼ cup into the center of each dough round and spread around evenly while leaving a very thin border. Drizzle the top with a little olive oil and season with salt and pepper. (You will add the herbs after the pizzettes come out of the oven.)

Ricotta Pizzettes Topping

Extra-virgin olive oil for brushing drizzling

1 cup fresh whole-milk ricotta, drained well*

Flaky sea salt, such as Maldon, for seasoning

Freshly ground black pepper for seasoning

½ cup chopped mixed fresh herbs, such as basil, parsley, chervil, and tarragon

Black Olive and Anchovy Topping

Extra-virgin olive oil for brushing and drizzling

4 oil-packed anchovies, drained and kept whole (about ½ can)

½ cup black olives, such as niçoise

Fresh oregano leaves from 2 sprigs

Flaky sea salt, such as Maldon, for seasoning

If you are buying ricotta made in small batches and packed in baskets, it may not need to be drained as much as regular ricotta sold in plastic tubs.

For the black olive and anchovy pizzettes, place 1 anchovy in the center of each dough round. Scatter olives around the anchovy and sprinkle some oregano leaves on top. Finish with a pinch of salt.

Bake one pan at a time for 10 to 12 minutes, rotating once, or until the crusts and the bottoms are get nicely gold. If you are using a pizza stone, this may take only 8 minutes. Serve warm or at room temperature. Before serving the ricotta pizza, top it with the fresh herbs.

**If your oven can get as hot as 550°F, you can bake the pizzettes at that temperature for a crispier finish. Monitor the pan as it bakes so the parchment paper doesn't burn.

Some of my most treasured wine souvenirs are the memories of tasting something extraordinary, the kind of thing that makes the world stop around me, if only for a second. This is what happened when I first tasted Chemin Faisant, a wine made by Jean Delobre of La Ferme des Sept Lunes (The Farm of Seven Moons).

Everything about that night is clear to me. I was working at Le Dauphin, and although it was always busy, this night was exceptionally so. Early in the day, we had unboxed a new wine that I had been curious about, but I hadn't had the opportunity to taste it. That evening, while I was

juggling a million little things, I had a chat with a couple of regulars sitting at the bar. Because I knew they were very free about what they liked to drink, I grabbed the new wine for them to try.

As soon as I opened the bottle and smelled the cork, I knew it was going to be special. Usually sniffing a cork is just a precautionary thing—the cork should smell like cork, indicating a healthy wine. Sniffing a cork won't tell you much about what the wine will taste like, but on this occasion, the aroma of the cork went straight into my brain—I couldn't believe how good it smelled. Even though I probably paused for only a few seconds, it felt as if all the chaos around me had stopped. I knew I needed to taste this wine.

Made in Saint-Joseph, an appellation in the northern Rhône, the *sans soufre* (unsulfured) wine imparted an elegant, fruity expression of black olive and was concentrated but not overly strong. It had body and structure, but not too much of either. Yet it was more than all that, and ever since that first taste, this cuvée has delighted me every year. While it is wonderful when young, it is designed to be set aside for a while, allowing it to go deeper into the flavors of the Syrah grape. This wine has not only become iconic to me, but it's also a tribute to how, even in the middle of a maddening day, a special wine can capture our attention and make a memory that lasts forever.

CLAMS AND SMOKED SAGE BUTTER

When I was a kid, my parents took me and my brother on vacation to Île d'Oléron, an island off of the Atlantic coast. When the tide went out, all of these little clams called *tellines* (wedge clams), stayed behind, and we could forage for them by raking the sand. My brother and I loved collecting clams so much that nearly every day my mum would cook up a pot of clams with a bit of butter and a bunch of fresh herbs. The clams were so tiny that they didn't really create enough for dinner, but they were perfect for eating directly out of the pot. I started thinking about clams more recently while at Clamato, a restaurant from chef Bertrand Grébaut of Septime. There, they were serving little clams in a butter made with Vin jaune from Jura. While I have no clue how they made this incredible butter, the dish reminded me how delicious something as simple as clams could be.

Clams are perfect for *apéro*: instead of shelling pistachios, you can "shell" and pop them in your mouth. But while I am still partial to finding the smallest clams I can find, larger clams work as well. Offer bread on the side to soak up the extra buttery sauce.

Soak the clams in cold salted water for several minutes (this will make them spit out any sand). Drain and repeat. If the clams are really sandy (which is often the case when you forage them yourselves), you may have to do this several times until the soaking water is no longer sandy. Give them a rinse before proceeding.

CONTINUED

SERVES 4 (AS AN APPETIZER)

3 pounds clams, such as littlenecks or Manila

2 tablespoons Burnt Sage Butter (page 74) or other flavored butter*

¼ cup white wine

Pinch of flaky sea salt, such as Maldon

My favorite butter to use for this recipe is Burnt Sage Butter (page 74), but regular Sage Butter (page 74) and Seaweed Butter (page 71) work perfectly, too. If you are short a flavored butter, opt for a high-quality salted butter.

Heat a dry pot over high heat for 1 minute. Add the clams, cover the pot, and cook, shaking the pot occasionally, until all the clams are opened, about 2 minutes for small clams and 4 minutes for larger clams. Uncover the pot. The clams should have made their own liquid in the pan as they cooked; discard any clams that don't open. Add the butter, wine, and salt and mix everything together until the butter is completely melted.

Using a slotted spoon, scoop the clams into a warmed bowl. Simmer the juices for 2 to 3 minutes more to concentrate the flavors a bit further. With a fine-mesh strainer, strain the juices left in the pot over the clams (this is to catch any extra bits of sand or pieces of shell) and serve immediately.

CHICKEN IN HAY

One of my most memorable meals from chef Alain Passard was actually not at L'Arpège but at one of his *potagers* (kitchen gardens). Our group sat in the shade of the patio for a beautiful lunch of lamb and beef grilled in the fireplace by the chef himself. By the end of the meal, we were so full and sleepy from the food and wine that we laid down on the grass before getting up the energy to battle a mischievous goat for the best wild strawberries in the garden. Yet even though I know I am lucky to have that *potager* experience and fortunate to have enjoyed lunch at L'Arpège on more than one occasion, there has always been one Alain Passard dish that I have never been able to try: chicken in hay. I loved the artistry of the idea (cooking a chicken in what looks like a nest) and nostalgia for the aroma of dried grass that reminds me of my childhood in the countryside. The times I've been to L'Arpège, however, it's never been "chicken in hay" day, which only made me dream about eating this dish even more. I became so obsessed that I was motivated to make my own humble version.

In his recipe, Alain Passard cooks the chicken in a cocotte sealed with dough in the oven. Since my oven has always been too small to fit a cocotte, I cook mine slowly on the stove, which allows the aroma of hay to fill my apartment.

CONTINUED

SERVES 4 TO 6

1 (3- to 4-pound) chicken, innards removed, trussed if possible*

1½ teaspoons fine sea salt

½ teaspoon freshly ground black pepper

1 tablespoon extra-virgin olive oil

5 to 6 handfuls organic hay (about 12 cups)**

2 cups water

Flaky sea salt, such as Maldon, for seasoning

*Maybe it's because I'm French, but I always use a trussed chicken (my butcher ties it for me). However, this preference is mainly an aesthetic one and you can cook the chicken untrussed just the same.

**I gather hay on visits to the countryside, but it is also available at pet stores that sell it for rabbits, guinea pigs, and other small animals. Ensure that the hay is organic before cooking with it. If you are friendly with a farmer at your local market, you may ask them if they have any hay they can supply you with. The hay is only for flavoring the chicken, not for eating.

Take the chicken out of the refrigerator and pat dry. Season all over, including the insides, with salt and pepper, then massage the whole chicken with olive oil. Let sit at room temperature for 1 hour so the chicken will cook more evenly.

In a 6- to 7-quart (or similar size) cocotte or Dutch oven, cover the bottom of the pan with about 3 inches of hay. Nestle the chicken in the center and arrange the hay on the sides so the chicken looks as if it's sitting in a nest. Place the cocotte over high heat for 1 to 2 minutes, then pour in the water. The pan should start to steam. (If it doesn't, keep heating it.) Cover the cocotte, lower the heat to medium-low, and cook for 30 minutes.

Remove the lid and check the base of the cocotte to make sure there is still water on the bottom to prevent the hay from burning. Return the lid and continue to cook for 30 to 40 minutes more, or until one of the chicken thighs is tender when pierced with a knife. At this point, the hay will have turned from a light greenish yellow to a deeper yellow-brown color, but it should never burn. If you are worried that the hay is close to scorching, lower the heat to low and add ½ cup water. The fewer times you remove the lid to check the chicken, the more evenly it will cook, but a peek now and again to check progress is perfectly fine.

Cut off the butchers' twine (if trussed) and discard. For the most impressive statement, serve the chicken in the hay nest at the table and carve it directly in the cocotte (if this feels too cavalier, put the chicken on a cutting board). Cut the legs off and serve, breast meat off of the breast bone as best as you can and slice it. Serve, offering flaky sea salt at the table.

BACK FROM BELLEVILLE PORK RÔTI

I go to the Asian grocery stores that surround the Belleville Métro station at least twice a month to stock up on rice vinegar, soba, and instant miso soup for home. On these visits, I look for ingredients that are new to me, from herbs I've never tried to I-don't-know-what sold in a beautiful tin (to be honest, sometimes I buy things for the packaging). I come home and ask myself, "What is this? Is it just green tea?" Then I try to figure out what to do with these new ingredients. While not all of my trials are a success, some can be quite good. One day, I purchased shiso leaves, which have beautiful scalloped edges and an herbal-spicy flavor. To use them, I came up with the idea to cover the exterior of a pork rôti (roast) with the leaves and cook it in a sweet-sour sauce—and the result has become one of my favorite Belleville-inspired experiments.

Take the pork out of the refrigerator 1 hour before cooking. If the butcher has tied twine around it, snip it off (you will add new twine later). Season the meat with salt and pepper

If any of the shiso leaves have long, tough stems, trim them off. Cover the sides of the pork completely with overlapping shiso leaves, leaving the ends exposed.

Cut four pieces of twine long enough to go around the sides of the roast and then use the pieces to tie up the roast. (This helps keep the leaves in place as the pork cooks: it does not have to be perfectly tied). Tuck the dried chile or green peppercorn clusters under one of the strings on top.

In a 6- to 7-quart (or similar size) cocotte or Dutch oven over medium heat, stir together the ketchup, vinegar, soy sauce, honey, ginger, and water and bring to a simmer over medium heat.

Put the roast into the cocotte, bring the sauce back to a simmer, and then turn the heat to low. Cover and cook over low heat for 45 to 55 minutes until the roast springs back only slightly when you press the top of it or the internal temperature reaches 145°F, (the internal temperature will continue to rise as the meat rests). Check a few

SERVES 5

2½ pounds boneless center-cut pork loin roast

1 teaspoon fine sea salt

½ teaspoon freshly ground black pepper

15 large or 30 small shiso leaves (it's better to have more than not enough)

1 dried red chile or 3 fresh green peppercorn clusters (optional)

¾ cup ketchup

¼ cup unseasoned rice vinegar

2 tablespoons soy sauce

1 tablespoon honey

1 heaping tablespoon grated fresh ginger

½ cup water

Have butchers' twine on hand to tie up the roast to keep the shiso leaves in place. The pork and its sauce has enough flavor that I often just serve this with white sticky rice. Leftover pork can be sliced for a sandwich: add a little bit of the sauce to the bread with some pickles and crisp lettuce.

times during the cooking process to make sure the sauce is gently simmering with only a few bubbles on the sides, not boiling.

Let the pork rest in the cooking juices for 15 to 20 minutes to let the meat relax and reabsorb some of its juices. Transfer the pork to a cutting board and cover with aluminum foil to keep warm.

Bring the sauce to a brisk simmer and cook until the sauce thickens enough to lightly coat the back of a spoon, about 4 minutes, though it could be less time depending on how tight the lid fits and how much liquid the pork released.

For the most impressive presentation, put the pork back into the cocotte and present it whole so everyone can see it. Then snip the strings off of the roast and peel them away before slicing and serving (if some of the leaves come off with the strings, pat them back in place). Ensure everyone gets some of the sauce with the pork.

BEEF STEW IN WINE AND ORANGE PEEL

My mum used to make us this stew with pork cheeks because they were inexpensive at the time and also crazy delicious, the pork becoming completely tender during the long cooking process. I have since made it with pork cheeks, beef cheeks, and the kinds of braising cuts used for *bœuf bourguignon*, and they all work well. With pork, the stew is lighter and more tender and with beef it takes on a deeper, richer flavor, but the flavors of orange and sweet wine complement both versions. My favorite uses beef cheeks, which add so much body to the braising liquid; it's really a magical cut of meat. The big difference between using beef cheeks and other cuts of beef is time: the cheeks have to cook much longer before they become tender. (They also may require a special order from the butcher's shop, but they are worth trying.) I love serving this stew with large shell pasta because the pasta catches the braising juices.

In a large bowl, season the meat with fine sea salt and pepper. Add the wine with the rosemary, sage, bay leaf, the peel of 2 of the oranges and the juice of 1 of the oranges and marinate in the refrigerator for at least 3 hours or overnight. Drain the meat, but reserve the marinade, discarding only the herbs and orange peel.

Warm 1 tablespoon of the olive oil in a large skillet over medium-high heat. In batches to avoid crowding the pan, sear the meat on all sides until evenly browned, about 8 minutes per batch. The meat may start to char a bit, but that's okay—just lower the heat as needed and drizzle in a little more oil. Transfer the browned meat to a plate and start on the next batch.

In a 6- to 7-quart (or similar size) cocotte or Dutch oven, heat the remaining 1 tablespoon olive oil over medium heat. Stir in the onion and garlic and cook, stirring often, until the onion has softened, about 4 minutes. Add the marinade and bring to a simmer over medium

SERVES 4 TO 6

3 pounds stewing beef, cut into 1-inch pieces*

1 tablespoon fine sea salt

½ teaspoon freshly ground black pepper

1 (750-ml) bottle sweet wine, such as Muscat or Banuyls**

1 sprig rosemary

1 sprig sage

1 bay leaf

3 oranges, preferably organic

2 tablespoons extra-virgin olive oil, or more if needed

1 yellow onion, finely diced

2 garlic cloves, minced

2 tablespoons salted butter

1 tablespoon honey

4 carrots, thinly sliced crosswise

Flaky sea salt, such as Maldon, for seasoning

heat. Cook for 10 minutes to infuse the flavors, then strain the marinade, discarding the onion and garlic.

Return the cocotte to the stove and melt the butter with the honey over medium heat. Using a Microplane, grate the zest of the remaining orange into the cocotte, then stir in the carrots and a pinch of salt. Cook, stirring constantly, just until the edges of the carrots start to soften, 1 to 2 minutes.

Put the meat on top of the carrot layer and pour in enough of the marinade so that the meat is almost completely covered. Bring the liquid to a simmer over medium-high heat, then lower the heat to low and cover. Cook the stew gently, checking every so often to make sure the juices aren't boiling, for 2½ to 3 hours, until the meat is tender. If you're not sure, taste a small piece of beef to check if it is still chewy.

Let the stew rest in its juices for 20 minutes before serving to let it absorb more flavor. Alternatively, let the meat cool completely and refrigerate to serve the next day. (This will let the flavors deepen even more.) Reheat the stew gently on the stove, adding a little water if needed to loosen the sauce up.

*Beef chuck and top round are good choices. If using beef cheeks, use the same weight as called for in this recipe and cut each cheek into four pieces.

**When buying sweet wine, either white or red wines will work. A sweet wine, like Muscat, will make a lighter-colored sauce, while a sweet red wine, like Banyuls, will make a deeper-flavored stew. My mum used Banyuls, so that's what I tend to use. But please don't use your most special Banyuls ever (like the wine I talk about on page 200); something simple is fine. Some sweet wines are sold in 500 ml bottles; if that is the case, buy 2 bottles.

The first orange wine that I tasted came from northern Italy, and to be frank it was not something that I fell in love with. Orange wines are white wines made like red wines: the grapes and their skins and seeds macerate in their juices, often for quite some time. The skins of the white grapes give the wine a deeper color, and the result is a something that doesn't taste or look like either a white or a red. On that first sip, my brain didn't know what to think because the flavors and tannins were so unexpected.

My opinion did not change for years, even after attending a tasting of Georgian wines. I remember listening to people describe how these skin-contact wines were made in an ancestral way in terra cotta *qvevri* (the ancient Georgian style of amphora), which was fascinating. But even hearing about the history of the wine was not enough for me to fall for them. I still couldn't adjust to the earthy, rustic flavors and started to assume this style wasn't for me. I became an orange-wine skeptic.

It was only after encountering a wine at chef Simone Tondo's old restaurant Roseval in the 20ème (now closed) that I changed my mind. Roseval was my bar around the corner, my second home, my favorite place to go for a plate of Simone's pasta after my shift. Martin Ho, a sommelier from Copenhagen, had joined the restaurant and started bringing in new wines I hadn't tasted before. One night he had me try two white cuvées from an Austrian winemaker, one made with skin contact. For the first time, I saw how the maceration elevated the wine without becoming overpowering. Instead, the flavors extracted from the grape skins integrated into the wine. That this wine was actually orange was also a surprise: the color was much lighter than previous styles I had tried.

It wasn't long before this wine, Himmel auf Erden Maischevergoren (meaning the skin-contact bottling from his "heaven on earth" series of wines), from Christian Tschida, became the only wine I ordered at Roseval. I became a little obsessed with it, asking Martin to save bottles for me, while also getting all of my friends to taste it, too. Eventually, I was able to start buying the wine for La Buvette. Often when I become excited about a wine, I also make an effort to learn more about the winemaker. But at that point, even though I loved Himmel auf Erden, I had never met Christian. Then one day a guy was standing in front of La Buvette, seeming to assess the wines in the window. He came in, looked at every wine along the side wall, and ordered a slice of terrine and a glass of wine. For half an hour, he sat quietly, taking in every detail of the shop, until at last we started to chat. He finally told me he was the winemaker of one of the bottles I sold. I will let you imagine how thrilled I was to hear that.

I later invited him to pour his wines at a tasting I organized on the floor of the Théâtre des Bouffes du Nord, a century-old theater that was being restored. I was sure he would decline—he's not the kind of winemaker who likes to spend time away from his work. But he came in for the day just for the tasting, the first time he had taken part in an official tasting of his wines in Paris.

While that story is more about making a connection with a person than it is about the technical aspects of orange wine, the message is to taste with an open mind over whatever is popular.

LA BUVETTE

CHOU FARCI

This recipe for stuffed cabbage originated from the note-book of recipes my mum gave me when I moved to Paris to study Arabic. In the center of the notebook, she had placed a page from an old magazine featuring a recipe for *chou farci* alongside a photo of a French chef posing with a huge stuffed cabbage. To my mum, the recipe is important because it's one of the first things she cooked for my father. It took me years to get up the courage to make it, but I've since made it many times in several tiny Parisian kitch-ens without any special equipment except for my beloved cocotte. When I had been working at Le Chateaubriand for only a few weeks, I made the mistake of talking about my *chou farci*, which prompted Iñaki Aizpitarte to say, "So, when are you going to invite me to dinner?" "When can you come?" I asked. He accepted my invitation in the easiest and most chill way. Two seconds later, I thought to myself, "Oh my God, now I'm going to have to cook for Iñaki, a real chef!" So I made the *chou farci* exactly as I had made it before. Fortunately, he enjoyed it, and I was relieved.

To prepare the cabbage, fill a large pot halfway with water and add a couple of tablespoons of salt. Bring the water to a boil. Remove the outer leaves of the cabbage but save them (they will come in handy later when closing up the cabbage). Cut a cross into the stem end of the cabbage deep enough to help the thick stem end and center of the cabbage cook more evenly. Carefully lower the cabbage into the water and cook over high heat for 5 to 6 minutes or until the leaves have started to soften and become pliable. Using tongs or a slotted spoon, gently turn the cabbage over to cook the other side for another 5 to 6 minutes. In the last 2 minutes, add the reserved outer leaves. Drain the cabbage into a colander, run cold water over it briefly, and then let it sit in the colander at room temperature until cool enough to handle.

SERVES 6 TO 8

1 large savoy cabbage, 2½ to 3 pounds

2½ teaspoons fine sea salt, plus extra for seasoning the cabbage-cooking water

8 ounces caul fat*

White vinegar, or any kind of inexpensive vinegar for soaking the caul fat

1 large carrot, peeled

1 large yellow onion

2 pounds ground pork

1 cup chopped flat-leaf parsley

1 teaspoon freshly ground black pepper

1 tablespoon salted butter

1 tablespoon extra-virgin olive oil

1 cup water, or any vegetable or meat-based broth, for deeper flavor

Caul fat looks like a thin sheet of lace when unwrapped, and it is often sold frozen. If your nearby butcher shop does not have it, ask if they can order it for you. If you can't find caul fat, you can still make the stuffed cabbage, but tie an extra piece of twine around the perimeter of the cabbage to ensure everything holds together. When you're not using caul fat, don't tie the twine too tight, or it will cut into the cabbage leaves.

Meanwhile, soak the caul fat in a bowl of room-temperature water with a generous tablespoon of vinegar for about 5 minutes, then drain. Repeat this step a couple of times to remove any offal type of aroma.

To make the filling, use the large holes of a box grater to grate the carrot and onion. In a large bowl using your hands, mix together the grated vegetables, pork, parsley, pepper, and salt.

Before you start to stuff the cabbage, first picture the process of opening up the cabbage and then putting the pork filling in between the leaves while molding the cabbage back into its original round shape. Clear off a large space on the counter and spread out a kitchen towel. Put the cabbage in the center of the towel (the towel will absorb any extra water).

Pry open the cabbage and flatten out the leaves so they look like a petals of a flower. When you get to the core of the cabbage, which is about the size a bit smaller than a baseball, use a paring knife to carefully cut out the core and put a similar-sized ball of filling in its place. Cover the filling with the first layer of leaves (about 5 to 6) surrounding the center so it looks as if you're closing up the petals of the flower to make a cabbage ball. Pat a thin layer of meat around the outside of the leaves to cover them, then cover with another layer of leaves, followed with another layer of meat until all of the meat filling is used, keeping the last 5 or 6 largest leaves free so you can close up the cabbage properly without any meat exposed. If there is still some filling peeking out on the top of the cabbage, cover the gaps with the reserved outer leaves.

Stretch out the caul fat in a single layer. Put the cabbage on the caul fat facing down, then wrap the cabbage in caul fat until covered.

Cut a piece of butcher's twine long enough to fit around the circumference of the cabbage with room to spare. Cut three more pieces the same size, then tie the pieces in a knot in the center so when you fan the twine out, it looks like a star made of strings. Put the cabbage face-down onto the center of the twine star, then tie up

CONTINUED

the twine at the top of the cabbage to make it snug. If you have a friend in the kitchen, have them help hold the twine in place with their finger while you tie the knot. (The idea is that the twine acts like a basket holding the cabbage's shape while the caul fat partially melts away and flavors the dish.)

Heat the butter and oil in a 7-quart (or larger) cocotte or Dutch oven over medium heat. Gently place the cabbage face-up inside, then let it cook until it just starts to turn golden, about 3 minutes. Pour in the water, bring the water to a simmer, then lower the heat to as low as it will go and cover. Cook gently, basting with cooking juices 3 or 4 times and adding more water if the bottom looks dry, for 1 hour, or until the cabbage is tender and the meat is cooked throughout. Turn off the heat and let the cabbage rest for about 10 minutes to reabsorb some of the cooking juices before serving.

To serve, gently lift the cabbage out of the cocotte and place onto a platter. Cut away the twine and discard. Slice the cabbage into wedges and spoon some of the cooking juices on top.

DESSERT

I am never shy about ordering dessert—or sweet wine. Maybe it stems from being a kid eating bread and chocolate for *goûter*, but I think it's more because a special meal never feels complete unless there is something sweet at the end. Some of the best desserts can be the simplest, showing off the quality of the cream or fruit, while others can be a little richer, like crème caramel or chocolate mousse. These recipes I've shared here illustrate my love of classic bistro cuisine, especially dessert.

LA BUVETTE

FONTAINEBLEAU

Fontainebleau is a classic treat that you can find at a *crèmerie*, a traditional cheese shop. Made by blending fromage blanc and whipped cream, it's one of the few things that is prepared in the shop. The original recipe comes from the city of Fontainebleau and was driven by the desire to make fromage blanc lighter in texture. No one knows if the original recipe was made with whipped egg whites or whipped cream, but at some point, whipped cream became fashionable, and I've never seen a version that doesn't have it. The point of this simple dessert is showcasing the fragile balance between cheese and air, and a spoonful served in a bowl is as pure an expression of fresh dairy flavor as there is. It is also great with spoonful of jam.

In a chilled bowl with a hand-held electric mixer (or a whisk if you would like the exercise), whip the cream with the sugar until it forms soft peaks. Using a rubber spatula, fold in the fromage blanc until evenly incorporated. Cover and keep in the refrigerator until serving, or serve right away.

SERVES 2 TO 3 (MAKES ABOUT 2 CUPS)

1 cup heavy cream, chilled

3 tablespoons confectioners' sugar

½ cup fromage blanc*

Fromage blanc is a fresh cow's milk cheese with a subtle tangy flavor and silky texture. It is sold in a plastic tub. Look for it at well-stocked cheese counters.

RED-WINE POACHED PEARS

Poached pears can be an elegant dessert served simply, just on a plate alone or with a spoonful of freshly whipped cream. The typical version can be a bit too sweet, filled with vanilla and cinnamon. To counter the sweetness, I add a bit of pepper for more of a spiced edge. Timut pepper is quite unique in that it has a citrus aroma that also works well with the pears.

Choose a pot that will fit the pears snugly (this way they will stay more covered in liquid while cooking). Combine the wine, zest, peppercorns, and honey in the pot and bring to a simmer over medium-high heat. While the poaching liquid heats up, peel the pears carefully, keeping the whole shape and stem in tact.

Gently lower the pears into the poaching liquid. Bring the liquid back to a simmer over medium-high heat, then lower the heat to low. Cook, gently turning the pieces over 3 or 4 times during the process, until the pears are cooked through and tender but still hold their shape 35 to 40 minutes. Using a slotted spoon, transfer the pears out of the poaching liquid and onto a plate to cool. If any of the peppercorns stick to the pears, pick them out.

Bring the poaching liquid to a simmer over medium heat and cook until slightly thicker, with more concentration of flavor, about 10 minutes. Strain.

Cool the cooking liquid and pears to room temperature, then combine the two together, cover, and refrigerate for a least 1 hour, or up to 3 days. Serve the pears chilled in a bowl with a spoonful of the poaching liquid.

SERVES 4

1 (750 ml) bottle ripe red wine, such as Valpolicella or Zinfandel

4 strips orange or grapefruit zest

½ teaspoon timut peppercorns*

¼ cup honey

4 medium pears, preferably slightly underripe

*If you can't find timut peppercorns, look for sansho peppercorns. If both are impossible to find, use black peppercorns.

LA BUVETTE

Panna Cotta

When I was living in my tiny student flat in a Paris suburb while attending university, my kitchen wasn't much more than a sink and an electric burner. These restrictions didn't stop my mum from giving me a small cookbook about panna cotta, which was part of a series of cookbooks by a French publisher covering every European classic you could think of—tarte tatin, macarons, quiches, and so on. In my limited kitchen, panna cotta was the perfect thing to make: all I needed was something for heating cream and a refrigerator. Inspired by the book, I made a lot of panna cotta in that tiny kitchen, and even today I can't resist experimenting, trying out different versions.

Because it's hard for me to pick a favorite, I share two base recipes and offer a couple of different ways to add flavor. Neither of them are very sweet, which helps the true taste of the dairy come through. One features cream, which I infuse with either rosemary sprigs or Dried Mandarin Peels (page 68). The second is tangier and made with buttermilk and goat yogurt, a version inspired by the panna cotta that chef Guillaume Rouxel used to make at Le Dauphin when I worked there. I like to finish this version with a sprinkle of Sage Dust (pictured on page 73), but it is also fine without it. Instead of unmolding the panna cotta onto a plate to serve it, I serve the dessert in what it's set in, either one large bowl or in a handful of small ceramics, saucers, jam jars, or anything that looks nice and will fit in the refrigerator.

CONTINUED

CLASSIC PANNA COTTA

In a small pot over medium-high heat, warm the cream and sugar, stirring occasionally, until the sugar dissolves and small bubbles form on the edge of the cream, about 2 minutes. Add either the rosemary or mandarin peels and bring the cream nearly to a boil over high heat, about 2 minutes more. Turn off the heat and let the cream sit for 10 minutes to infuse the flavors.

Soak the gelatin sheets in ice water to hydrate them for about 5 minutes.

Remove and discard the rosemary or mandarin peel and bring the cream to a simmer over medium heat for 1 minute. Squeeze out the extra water from the gelatin and add the gelatin to the cream, stirring with a whisk or rubber spatula until dissolved.

Pour the panna cotta into one large bowl or use six small bowls and pour ½ cup into each one. Let the cream cool to room temperature, then refrigerate until set, at least 5 hours or preferably overnight. (This panna cotta sets softer than some recipes, but the flavor of the dairy comes through better.) Panna cotta keeps for 3 days in the refrigerator, though it may become firmer as it sits.

SERVES 6

3 cups heavy cream

3 tablespoons sugar

2 to 3 rosemary sprigs, or
4 Dried Mandarin Peels
(page 68) (optional)

2 gelatin sheets*

Gelatin sheets are also sometimes called leaf gelatin; look for them at specialty pastry shops or online.

GOAT YOGURT PANNA COTTA

Soak the gelatin sheets in ice water to hydrate them for about 5 minutes.

In a pot over medium-high heat, warm the cream with the sugar, stirring occasionally until the sugar dissolves and tiny bubbles form on the edges of the cream, about 2 minutes. Squeeze out the extra water from the gelatin and add the gelatin to the cream, stirring with a whisk or rubber spatula until dissolved. Let cool for 10 minutes, then stir in the buttermilk and goat yogurt.

Pour the panna cotta base into one large bowl or use eight small bowls and pour ½ cup into each one. Refrigerate until set, at least 3 hours or preferably overnight. Panna cotta keeps for 3 days in the refrigerator, though it may become slightly firmer as it sits.

SERVES 8

3 gelatin sheets (see note opposite page)

2 cups heavy cream

¼ cup sugar

1 cup buttermilk, at room temperature

1 cup plain goat yogurt, at room temperature*

Having the buttermilk and yogurt at room temperature before adding it to the warm panna cotta base prevents the water and solids in the yogurt from separating as the panna cotta sets.

CRÈME CARAMEL

Chef Léa Fleuriot and her brother, Louis Fleuriot, opened Le Cadoret at the end of 2017, and it has since become one of my favorite bistros in Paris. Since I work in the evenings, I mostly go for the short lunch menu, which always ends with a classic dessert. Before running a kitchen of her own, Léa worked at many restaurants in Paris, including two months at Yohan Lastre's restaurant, Lastre Sans Apostrophe. It was here where she encountered her favorite version of crème caramel, which was made for the staff lunch. Léa thought this was crazy—this crème caramel was too delicious to be enjoyed only by the staff! At Le Cadoret, she uses that memory for inspiration for her own version. As with the original recipe, Léa bakes it in one large ceramic bowl instead of individual ramekins, allowing her to serve the crème caramel in creamy, generous scoops.

Adjust the oven rack to the lower-middle position and preheat to 325°F. Have ready a 9 by 13-inch baking dish and a 2-quart round or oval baking dish that fits inside of it (a glass or ceramic bowl works well). The baking dish will hold water, insulating the crème caramel from the heat of the oven. Also have a kettle of hot water ready.

To make the caramel, in a saucepan over medium heat, stir the sugar and water together with a rubber spatula until the sugar is completely wet and has started to melt. After a minute, stop stirring and watch the pan, swirling it occasionally, until the sugar begins to turn golden in color, about 5 minutes. After that, the sugar will start to brown quickly. Once it reaches a golden-amber color, turn off the heat and pour the sugar into the 2-quart casserole. Let cool.

To make the custard, pour the milk into a separate pot. Use a spoon to scrape out the vanilla bean seeds, then add the seeds and bean to the milk. Bring the milk to a boil over high heat, turn off the heat, and let the vanilla steep into the milk for 15 minutes. Remove the vanilla bean from the milk.

CONTINUED

SERVES 8 GENEROUSLY

Caramel

¾ cup sugar

2 tablespoons water

Custard

4 cups whole milk

1 vanilla bean, halved lengthwise

4 whole eggs

8 egg yolks

½ cup sugar

LA BUVETTE

In a large bowl, whisk together the eggs, yolks, and sugar until light yellow. Whisk the milk, 1 cup at a time into the eggs until creamy and thoroughly combined.

Pour the custard over the caramel and put the casserole in the baking dish. Gently place the baking dish in the oven and then carefully pour hot water from the kettle into the baking dish until the water reaches halfway up the sides of the casserole. Bake until the center of the custard is just barely set and the top has turned a deep cream color and doesn't stick to your finger when touched, about 1 hour depending on the depth of the casserole (a shallower pan could be done in less time; a deeper pan could take up to 1 hour and 15 minutes).

Carefully lift the casserole out of the water and let the custard cool to room temperature, about 1½ hours. Cover the top with plastic wrap and refrigerate until cold, at least 2 hours or overnight.

To serve, scoop crème caramel into bowls, drizzling some of the caramel sauce that forms at the bottom of the custard over the top to finish. Leftover crème caramel keeps for 3 days in the refrigerator.

PÂTE SABLÉE

I use the same pâte sablée (a classic short pastry dough used to make tarts) for my berry tart (page 194) as I do for my lemon meringue tart (facing page), so if you want to make both desserts, double the recipe. Before you start, have a 9-inch tart pan with a removable base ready.

To make the pâte sablée, in a bowl with a spatula, smash together the butter, almond flour, and sugar. Add the all-purpose flour gradually and mix it in with your hands, kneading it until a crumbly dough forms. Add the egg yolk and water and gently mix with your hands until the dough comes together. Shape the dough into a disk. If the dough is sticking to your hands, sprinkle with a little more all-purpose flour and continue to shape the dough. Cover with plastic wrap and refrigerate it for at least 2 hours, or overnight.

To bake the tart crust, preheat the oven to 350°F. Dust the counter with flour.

Using a rolling pin or empty wine bottle, roll out the dough until it is a circle about 11 inches wide. (You need enough dough to cover the bottom and the sides of the tart pan.) Place the dough into the tart pan, pressing it into the sides of the tart so it is completely covered. Using a paring knife, cut off any overhanging dough so all sides of the tart are even. Poke little holes across the base of the dough with a fork. (If the room is very warm or the dough feels sticky, put the pan in the refrigerator to chill for 10 minutes before proceeding.) Put a piece of parchment paper on top of the dough and weigh it down with pie weights or dried beans (you just need something to keep the crust from rising up as it bakes).

Bake for 15 minutes. Remove the weights and paper, return to the oven, and bake until the pastry is a nice golden color, 15 to 18 minutes (it is better to overbake it slightly than to underbake it). Let the tart shell cool completely.

MAKES ONE 9-INCH
TART SHELL

½ cup salted butter, at room temperature

⅓ cup almond flour

½ cup confectioners' sugar

1 cup plus 2 tablespoons all-purpose flour

1 egg yolk*

1 tablespoon water

*If making ahead for the Lemon Meringue Tart, save the egg white for the meringue.

LEMON MERINGUE TART

When I lived in Paris as a student, I was taken to a *salon de thé* (tea parlor) by a friend who knew Paris a bit more than I did at the time. Le Loir dans la Thérière (The Dormouse in the Teapot) was the kind of place where you could spend the whole afternoon drinking tea and eating cake, which made it popular with students. This *salon de thé* was especially known well-known for its *tarte au citron* crowned with a seemingly disproportionate mountain of meringue. There is something special about lemon tarts that I've always loved, but the meringue in this version makes it even more impressive. Years later, I asked my mum for a lemon tart recipe, and she sent me one from Philippe Conticini, a famous pastry chef. My own version builds on that recipe, but I add a meringue tower as a tribute to those afternoons spent at Le Loir dans la Thérière. For this reason, the recipe uses 5 whole eggs: 1 yolk for the tart shell, 4 yolks for the curd, and five whites for the meringue.

To make the lemon curd, in a medium saucepan, melt the butter over low heat and remove from the heat. In a bowl, whisk the sugar with the egg yolks until well mixed. While whisking, pour the melted butter into the sugar-yolk mixture and then return everything to the saucepan. Stir in the lemon juice and zest. Cook over low heat, stirring constantly with a rubber spatula and ensuring that you stir from the bottom of the pot, until the curd starts to thicken enough to lightly coat the spatula, 7 to 9 minutes. (Make sure it never boils, or the eggs will become grainy; if it looks grainy, consider passing it through a sieve.) You will have about 1 cup.

Pour the lemon curd into a bowl and let cool to room temperature, about 1 hour, or refrigerate in a sealed container overnight. (You can also refrigerate the egg whites needed for the meringue in a separate sealed container; just bring them to room temperature before whipping them.)

CONTINUED

MAKES ONE 9-INCH TART, SERVES ABOUT 8

Lemon Curd

6 tablespoons salted butter

½ cup sugar

4 egg yolks

6 tablespoons freshly squeezed lemon juice

3 tablespoons finely grated lemon zest

*Meringue**

5 egg whites

Pinch of fine sea salt

1¼ cups sugar

Baked tart shell (Pâte Sablée, facing page)

A crème brûlée torch is the easiest way to brown the top of the meringue, but you can also use the broiler. If using a broiler, preheat it while making the meringue.

LA BUVETTE

To make the meringue, with a hand-held electric mixer on medium speed, whisk the whites with a pinch of salt until they form soft peaks and are fluffy, about 3 minutes. Add the sugar, 1 tablespoon at a time, while whisking, until the meringue looks shiny and is thick enough to form stiff peaks when the beaters are lifted out of the bowl, 3 to 5 minutes more.

Pour the cooled lemon curd into the tart shell and use a spatula to smooth out the surface into an even layer. Pile the meringue on top to make dramatic peaks.

Using a crème brûlée torch or the broiler setting in the oven, brown the top of the meringue until brown in parts (this could take 3 to 5 minutes in an oven under a broiler, but keep an eye on it the whole time). Cool to room temperature before cutting into the tart to serve.

WHIPPED CREAM AND BERRY TART

For me, perfection is fresh strawberries in season. When I walk by a shop and pass perfect strawberries, the smell of them jumps into my nose and I know it's truly springtime. This tart is about celebrating that idea of fresh berries, starting with strawberries, and then changing to raspberries or a combination of berries, whatever is in season and perfect to eat at that moment. For the best results, wait to fill the tart until you are ready to serve it so the crust doesn't soften.

Pat the berries dry. If using strawberries, hull them and cut in half, if large.

Right before serving, in a chilled bowl with a hand-held electric mixer (or a whisk if you would like the exercise), whip the cream with the mascarpone until soft peaks form. Add the sugar and the seeds scraped out of the vanilla bean half, then gently whisk together just until incorporated. Spoon the cream into the tart shell and place the berries on top. Serve right away.

MAKES ONE 9-INCH
TART, SERVES ABOUT 8

2 cups berries, the freshest you can find, gently washed

1 cup heavy cream

¾ cup mascarpone

3 tablespoons confectioners' sugar

½ vanilla bean

Baked tart shell (Pâte Sablée, page 190)

194

A CLASSIC CHOCOLATE MOUSSE

Chocolate mousse is one of the most classic bistro desserts, and I have loved it since I was a kid. This recipe comes from Trish Deseine's book *Je Veux du Chocolat!*, which became like a bible for chocolate lovers in France. For the best results, use your favorite kind of rich, dark chocolate, and plan on making it at least two hours or the day before serving so it has time to set. I love to scoop mousse onto small plates to serve, but this step was always impossible for my mum because my family would begin eating it directly out of the bowl before she could stop us. When I have any leftover mousse, I eat it the next day on bread, a tribute to childhood memories of *le goûter*.

Bring a pot of water to barely a simmer and set a heatproof bowl over it, making sure the bottom of the bowl doesn't touch the water. Combine the chocolate and butter in the bowl to melt. Once melted, turn off the heat, put the bowl on the counter to cool slightly, and stir the chocolate and butter together.

In a separate bowl, using a whisk or a hand-held electric mixer, beat the cream and sugar until the cream is light and fluffy. (Because this is a small amount of cream, this will happen quickly. Avoid over-whipping or the cream will turn grainy.)

In a separate large bowl, whisk the egg yolks until smooth. Using a rubber spatula, fold the whipped cream into the yolks, then fold in the melted chocolate mixture, trying to keep as much of the volume of the cream as possible.

In another large bowl, using a whisk or hand-held electric mixer on medium speed, whip the egg whites until the whites hold soft peaks when the beaters are lifted out of the bowl, 3 to 4 minutes. Gently fold the whites into the chocolate mixture until evenly combined but still light. Cover the bowl (or transfer into a serving bowl before covering), and refrigerate for least a couple of hours before serving to let it firm up.

SERVES 3 OR 4

7 ounces dark chocolate, chopped

3 tablespoons salted butter

½ cup heavy cream

3 tablespoons confectioners' sugar

3 eggs, separated

MULLED WINE

Many say they don't like mulled wine, but what they don't like is bad mulled wine. When you take time to put it together with care, you can make a lot of people happy. When I've prepared it for events at La Buvette or at Le Food Market, an outdoor market in Paris founded by my friend Virginie Godard, or even in my friend's shop for a special event, I found that it's quite popular. Part of it is nostalgia: the aroma takes people back to childhood and the idea that Christmas is right around the corner.

Mix all of the ingredients together in a pot and bring to a simmer over medium-high heat. Lower the heat to medium-low and gently cook until the wine is aromatic and flavorful, about 20 minutes. Taste, adding more honey, if desired. Ladle into heatproof glasses or mugs to serve. The longer the wine sits, the stronger the spices will become.

SERVES 4 TO 5

1 (750 ml) bottle ripe red wine, such as Valpolicella or Zinfandel*

¼ cup honey, or more to taste

¼ cup Cointreau or Grand Marnier

1 large thumb-sized piece of ginger, halved and smashed a bit (peeling optional)

1 star anise

3 cloves

3 cardamom pods, slightly smashed

½ cinnamon stick (or keep whole if it is too hard to break in half)

*I use something that is not sweet like a dessert wine but has the idea of sweetness— it's a sunny, ripe expression of a particular grape. It's even good if the wine tastes a little bit overripe. A concentrated Montepulciano from Italy or deep red wine from the South of France or even a California Zinfandel can all work. If you have any Dried Mandarin Peels (page 68), add them here for a delicate citrus accent.

When someone wants one more bottle to end a special evening at La Buvette, they often ask me to recommend something totally unexpected. This is when I suggest Manuel di Vecchi's Banyuls, a wine I love so much that I save the bottles to use as water carafes. "Sweet wine— really?" they ask. And then I convince them by explaining the story of this wine.

When Manuel decided to make this cuvée, he wanted it to be exceptional from start to finish. Sweet wines are a bit of a grandma thing, but they are also an important part of the tradition of Banyuls, a very warm area near the border with Spain where vines grow on terraced hillsides facing the Mediterranean. What makes this one so special is that everything—from picking and crushing the grapes to making the glass and bottling the wine—is done by hand. Even if he wanted to use machines to harvest the grapes, he wouldn't be able to—the terraces of old Grenache Noir vines are so steep that only humans can pick the fruit. Wind from the sea blows through the old vines, protecting them from mildew while also cooling the grapes from the powerful sun and preserving the freshness of the fruit.

The grapes are then crushed by foot in the smallest press you'll ever see—only two people fit inside. It's like a puppeteer's house, with everything made in miniature. A neighbor was a glass blower, so Manuel worked with him to make the bottles just for this wine. He also labels the bottles by hand. This is one of the reasons that I save them—the bottles are just as beautiful as the wine. None of this story would matter if I didn't like how the wine tastes. Despite the sugar left in the wine (a grape spirit

is added to stop the wine from fermenting dry), it has a nice freshness, which is unexpected for the usual ripe expression of fruit from this terroir. To me, opening this bottle, either to drink with blue cheese or just with one square of really great dark chocolate is an exceptional way to end a meal. You don't need much more than that.

ACKNOWLEDGMENTS

Emily Timberlake, for the unforgettable lunch that started everything

—

Etienne Legrand, for being not only irreplaceable but also the only person I know who can eat rillettes six days in a row

—

Mum, for sharing with me the taste of what's good

Dad, for sharing with me the taste of what's beautiful

—

Anna Polonsky for the rebirth of this book and becoming the best sister I could have dreamed of

—

Danièle Gérault for the education that changed my life

Christophe Lebègue for throwing the stone in the pond

Iñaki Aizpitarte for letting me work with without a three-day-old beard

FeGH for being the best godmother I could have dreamed of in Paris

Christine Muhlke, for being the best godmother I could have dreamed of in NYC

Gauthier Conan, for working so hard while I was out having fun making a book

—

My INCREDIBLE book team:

Kate Leahy

Marcus Nilsson

All my beloved and talented friends, cooks, & chefs, for their unconditional kindness & technical assistance:

Léa Fleuriot

Chloé Charles

Erica Archambault

Alix Lacloche

Tatiana Levha

Julie Della Faille

Chris & Christine Wilson

Daniel Baratier

Florent Ciccoli

Simone Tondo

Jeremy Lesaffre

—

Those who collaborated from near and far:

Jane Drotter

Nadine Decailly

Pauline Taboulet

Julie Heiligenstein & Gilles Plattner

Lucie Sorensen

Lola & Jeremie Kanza

Michelle, Christian & Carole Maurel

Tim Johnston, Margaux Johnston, & Romain Roudeaux

Benjamin Ageorges & Pauline Illiaquer

Gérard & Francoise Maquenheim

David Flynn & Thomas Lehoux

Cyril Bordarier

Kamel Tabti

Maxime Bardoux

Gilles Cachard

Christophe Fragnoli & Jacky Bethune

—

Assistance *litteraire & artistique:*

Caroline Goutal

Matthew Kay

James Casey

—

Kitty Cowles for being the great connector

—

The Ten Speed team:

Emma Rudolph

Lizzie Allen

Kelly Booth

Lorena Jones

Emma Campion

Jane Chinn

Andrea Chesman

Windy Dorresteyn

Allison Renzulli

Anne Goldberg

—

Those who helped with ingredients and recipes in the U.S.:

Sarah Henkin

Lulu Meyer

Jeanelle Hayner Olsen

—

Finally, to the community that has formed around the shop, from the Wednesday Club to the neighbors old and new, and to those of you who have traveled so far to share a moment at La Buvette

INDEX

Published in the United States by Ten Speed Press, an imprint of Random
House, a division of Penguin Random House LLC, New York.
www.tenspeed.com

Ten Speed Press and the Ten Speed Press colophon are registered
trademarks of Penguin Random House LLC.

Library of Congress Cataloging-in-Publication Data
Names: Fourmont, Camille, author. | Leahy, Kate, author.
Title: La Buvette : recipes and wine notes from Paris / by Camille Fourmont
    and Kate Leahy.
Description: First edition. | California ; New York : Ten Speed
    Press, 2020. | Includes bibliographical references and index.
Identifiers: LCCN 2019040994 |
Subjects: LCSH: Cooking, French. | Wine and wine
    making—France. | Buvette
    (Restaurant : Paris, France) | LCGFT: Cookbooks.
Classification: LCC TX719 .F76 2020 | DDC 641.5944—dc23
LC record available at https://lccn.loc.gov/2019040994

Hardcover ISBN: 978-1-9848-5669-2
eBook ISBN: 978-1-9848-5670-8

Printed in China

Design by Lizzie Allen

10 9 8 7 6 5 4 3 2 1